RETHINKING MILL'S ETHICS

RETHINKING MILL'S ETHICS
Character and Aesthetic Education

Colin Heydt

continuum
LONDON • NEW YORK

Continuum International Publishing Group
The Tower Building,
11 York Road,
London SE1 7NX

80 Maiden Lane
Suite 704
New York, NY 10038

© Colin Heydt 2006

All rights reserved. No part of this publication may be reproduced or transmitted in any form or by any means, electronic or mechanical, including photocopying, recording, or any information storage or retrieval system, without prior permission in writing from the publishers.

Colin Heydt has asserted his right under the Copyright, Designs and Patents Act, 1988, to be identified as Author of this work.

British Library Cataloguing-in-Publication Data
A catalogue record for this book is available from the British Library.

ISBN: 0-8264-86398 (Hardback)

Typeset by Fakenham Photosetting, Fakenham, Norfolk
Printed and bound in Great Britain by MPG Books Ltd, Bodmin, Cornwall

Contents

Acknowledgements

'There always will be murderers, tyrants, robbers, adulterers, plunderers, temple-thieves, traitors: worse than all these is the ungrateful man.'
(Seneca, *On Favours*, Book I)

The performance of duty, both by writer and editors, may well get books published, but it alone will rarely make the process pleasant. I have been the recipient of much goodwill, given even after duty's call was silent.

Seneca advises us to be discriminating about those to whom we look for favours. Whether it was judgement or luck that steered me in the direction I took, undoubtedly it steered me correctly. First and foremost, I must thank Knud Haakonssen, whose advice has been invaluable, and whose wit, patience, and sensible prodding has helped me in innumerable ways throughout the last few years. David Lyons, a second reader on the dissertation that eventually led to this book, brought a critical mind and sound counsel to this endeavour. It is a pleasure to acknowledge my debt to them.

This book began germinating in the Boston University philosophy department. A number of its professors influenced this work, directly or indirectly. In particular I would mention with thanks Henry Allison, Aaron Garrett, David Roochnik, Simon Keller, Juliet Floyd, the late Burton Dreben, Dan Dahlstrom and Alfredo Ferrarin.

My colleagues have left marks on this book from years of conversation and willingness to read half-finished writing. I would like to give special thanks to Matt Caswell and Darrin McMahon for commenting on earlier versions of Chapters 2 and 1, respectively, and to Lydia Moland, who brought her sharp mind (and sharp pen) to the assistance of many parts of the book that needed her help. They, along with Jim Boettcher, Jeff Holman, Marina McCoy, Linda Riviere and Mary Troxell, have been indispensable, both as colleagues and friends.

Scholars rarely, if ever, work outside the context of supportive institutions. This book would never have been produced without Boston University, the Institut für die Wissenschaften vom Menschen in Vienna, and Boston College. I am grateful for my involvement with each one.

Jim Feiser, the series editor at Continuum, was also instrumental in seeing this book to realization. Without his initial show of interest, other projects may have overwhelmed this one. Also at Continuum, Philip de Bary, Joanna Taylor and Anthony Haynes have been cheerful and efficient (not an inconsiderable virtue in the realm of academic publishing).

Lastly, I would like to thank my parents, John and Nancy Heydt, for their unwavering love and support, and my wife Stephanie, to whom this book is dedicated, for the 'meet and happy conversation' that makes things like writing books worth doing.

Chapter 1 is revised from its original appearance in *On Religion and Politics*, ed. C. Lovett and P. Kernahan (Vienna: IWM, 2004).

Earlier versions of Chapters 2 and 3 have been reprinted with the kind permission of the publishers of the *British Journal for the History of Philosophy* and the *Journal of the History of Philosophy*: Heydt, Colin. 'Narrative, Imagination, and the Religion of Humanity in Mill's Ethics'. *Journal of the History of Philosophy*, Volume XLIV, Number 1, January 2006, © Journal of the History of Philosophy, Inc. Reprinted with permission of The Johns Hopkins University Press.

Introduction

A number of philosophers in the eighteenth and nineteenth centuries rejected the idea that humans can make moral progress. Humanity's ethical character was not, on these accounts, amenable to basic alteration. Schopenhauer, for example, derided those with Promethean hopes for transforming humanity: 'Ethical writers ... who speak of a progress in virtue are always triumphantly refuted by reality and experience, which have demonstrated that virtue is inborn and cannot result from sermons. As something original, character is unchangeable.'[1] Such a position naturally tended to de-emphasize the importance of character education.

Optimistic thinkers, on the other hand, who are often seen as more representative of the mainstream of eighteenth- and nineteenth-century thought, took human nature to be improvable. John Stuart Mill's philosophy, for example, incorporates the possibility of limitless, though gradual, moral progress. And while Mill occasionally emphasizes the need for humility concerning what we can know about the best direction for human development ('experiments in living' often open up unanticipated possibilities), his Victorian propensity to moralize continually pushes him to provide pictures of what desirable lives look like and of how such lives are achieved.

Moral progress can be conceptualized in many different ways, of course, and it is the details that matter. For Mill, as Mandelbaum argues, moral improvement was 'primarily a matter of the cultivation of more complex—and, as he often said, *higher* and *nobler*—forms of feeling'. Though intellectual development was undoubtedly important, what truly transformed human nature was 'the manner in which experience affected the sensibilities of men. It increased the depth and the range of their social feelings, making them more sensitive to the rights and welfare of others, thereby causing that welfare to be a matter of immediate personal concern; and, in addition, it opened to them, for their own immediate pleasure, the more cultivated and complex forms of enjoyment of civilized men.'[2] Mill termed this cultivation of dispositions of feeling and imagination 'aesthetic education'. It is this type of education that improves our feelings of solidarity with others and that develops our capacities for various forms of higher pleasures and for living a more ennobled life. It is at the heart of Mill's sense of human possibility and it is the main subject of this book.

A stimulus for Mill's focus on aesthetic education was his concern about the existential impact of industrial modernity. It was especially during the early Victorian period that one finds among writers a growing self-consciousness of qualitative differences between older agrarian and newer industrial society. A number of thinkers, Mill included, thought that there were forces operating on individuals within a more industrialized and democratic society that tended to homogenize them and alienate them from one another. Since Mill had no interest in reactionary rejections of economic and social change, one of the ethical challenges that most absorbed him was how to foster feelings of solidarity and the cultivation of our humanity within modern society – that is, how to foster ethical development in a world that often seems to work against it. His views on aesthetic education reflect, among other things, his attempt to address this unprecedented challenge.

Given the centrality of aesthetic education for Mill's ethics, it has been surprisingly understudied. References to, let alone treatments of, aesthetic education are rare. This lack of sustained attention to the theme of the cultivation of feelings and imagination in Mill's ethics may be the result of ongoing attention to the more famous aspect of his theory, namely utilitarianism. Yet it is important to note from the outset that these themes are not separate. The focus on character development reflects his kind of utilitarianism. Mill did not think that the greatest aggregate happiness arose from a community in which people regularly and knowingly act on the basis of the principle of utility. People neither can nor should consistently direct their actions to achieving the end of increasing the overall happiness of all sentient beings. Thus the objective of education is not to transform people into agents who ever more self-consciously deliberate with the goal of improving overall happiness. The aim of education is, as we shall see, somewhat different.

This de-emphasis on the principle of utility's significance for deliberation can be found in Mill's criticism of Comte:

Why is it necessary that all human life should point but to one object, and be cultivated into a system of means to a single end? May it not be the fact that mankind, who after all are made up of single human beings, obtain a greater sum of happiness when each pursues his own, under the rules and conditions required by the good of the rest, than when each makes the good of the rest his only object, and allows himself no personal pleasures not indispensable to the preservation of his faculties? The regimen of a blockaded town should be cheerfully submitted to when high purposes require it, but is it the ideal perfection of human existence?[3]

Mill very consistently makes this claim. In *Utilitarianism*, he responds to critics who say that 'it is exacting too much to require that people shall always act from the inducement of promoting the general interest of society' by contending that 'this is to mistake the very meaning of a standard of morals and confound the rule of action with the motive of it'.[4]

That Mill minimizes the deliberative importance of the principle of utility and emphasizes that individuals can promote communal goods without any of them intending to do so should not be surprising when one remembers that Mill was an economist and the son of a Scot. A *locus classicus*[5] of this view is Adam Smith's *Wealth of Nations*:

[An individual] generally, indeed, neither intends to promote the publick interest, nor knows how much he is promoting it. By preferring the support of domestick to that of foreign industry, he intends only his own security; and by directing that industry in such a manner as its produce may be of the greatest value, he intends only his own gain, and he is in this, as in many other cases, led by an invisible hand to promote an end which was no part of his intention. Nor is it always the worse for the society that it was no part of it. *By pursuing his own interest he frequently promotes that of the society more effectually than when he really intends to promote it.* I have never known much good done by those who affected to trade for the publick good. It is an affectation, indeed, not very common among merchants, and very few words need be employed in dissuading them from it.[6]

Smith, however, is hardly the only source. One could cite thinkers going back at least as far as Mandeville, or even further if one looks at the history of providentialism, which contends that, often without realizing it, individuals play a role in furthering the greater good of God's creation

through attending to their own 'offices' or duties. A nice example of the
latter comes from a friend and patron of Smith's, Lord Kames:

> These several principles of action [love of life, self-love, the love of justice,
> gratitude, and benevolence] are ordered with admirable wisdom, to
> promote the general good, in the best and most effectual manner. We
> act for the general good, when we act upon these principles, even when
> it is not our immediate aim. The general good is an object too remote,
> to be the sole impulsive motive to action. It is better ordered, that, in
> most instances, individuals should have a limited aim, which they can
> readily accomplish. To every man is assigned his own task. And if every
> man do his duty, the general good will be promoted much more effec-
> tually, than if it were the aim in every single action.[7]

The notion, then, that the end of the greatest happiness, whereby we
judge an action to be good or bad, is often furthered most by actors who
do not intend to do so, had strong and influential precedents before Mill's
time.[8] Smith and Kames suggest that the unintentional promotion of the
general good is often more effective than the intentional because, even
where they are motivated by genuine goodwill, humans lack the capacity
to understand the whole with its complex interrelations of parts. This
limitation on our knowledge often generates unintended consequences
that, rather than improving things, make them worse.[9]

Beyond the problems of unintended consequences and of the difficulty
of knowing how to further very complex social ends through individual
actions, there are other justifications for strong scepticism about the use of
the principle of utility by individuals in most kinds of moral deliberation.
Firstly, Mill contends that there are a number of ways in which people
can be misled by the principle to attend to the wrong features of their
situation:

> As mankind are much more nearly of one nature, than of one opinion
> about their own nature, they are more easily brought to agree in their
> intermediate principles, *vera illa et media axiomata*, as Bacon says, than in
> their first principles: and the attempt to make the bearings of actions
> upon the ultimate end more evident than they can be made by referring
> them to the intermediate ends, and to estimate their value by a direct
> reference to human happiness, generally terminates in attaching most
> importance, not to those effects which are really the greatest, but to

those which can most easily be pointed to and individually identified. Those who adopt utility as a standard can seldom apply it truly except through the secondary principles.[10]

By examining actions with an eye to overall human happiness, we miss features of the action that may have important bearing for happiness but which may also be less readily noticed. Mill employs the example of murder: 'There are many persons to kill whom would be to remove men who are a cause of no good to any human being, of cruel physical and moral suffering to several, and whose whole influence tends to increase the mass of unhappiness and vice. Were such a man to be assassinated, the balance of traceable consequences would be greatly in favour of the act.'[11] Mill goes on to say, however, that this kind of action can help undermine the general rule not to kill, and if 'a hundred infringements would produce all the mischief implied in the abrogation of the rule, a hundredth part of that mischief must be debited to each one of the infringements, though we may not be able to trace it home individually. And this hundredth part will generally far outweigh any good expected to arise from the individual act.'[12] The 'traceable consequences', in other words, can easily mislead us into misconstruing an action's relation to the general good. As an empirical matter, we often attend to the wrong things in individual cases because we notice the most obvious consequences, not necessarily the most important ones.[13]

A final additional reason for scepticism regarding the desirability of the principle of utility guiding deliberation is that happiness is often best increased when individuals see it as their 'special business' to look after their own situation, because they understand it better and have greater power to affect it.[14] As moral development progresses, the happiness of the individual will increasingly depend on his/her care for and connection to others. Actions will more naturally be guided by others' concerns without the agent interpreting these actions as involving sacrifice. If one were to act consistently in a sacrificial manner, one would, perversely, tend to reduce overall happiness.

None of this constitutes an argument that Mill is a 'rule-utilitarian'. The basic proposition that Urmson put forward in his seminal paper arguing for a 'rule-utilitarian' interpretation of Mill's ethics – i.e. 'a particular action is justified as being right by showing that it is in accord with some moral rule' rather than by showing that it directly fosters overall happiness

– claims much more than I am claiming here.[15] Moreover, as an interpretation of Mill's overall moral theory, it is suggestive but not convincing. General rules are useful heuristics for imperfect deliberators, but they should not be depended upon exclusively. There are both decision contexts (e.g. legislative and jurisprudential) and individuals that correctly rely on the principle of utility as a deliberative principle. That is, in certain situations and with certain individuals, direct reliance on the principle of utility in deliberation will benefit the general good. What these contexts are, who these individuals are, and whether their number will increase with moral progress are all empirical questions – matters of trial and error.

If overall happiness is not best served by people regularly deliberating on the basis of the principle of utility, what kinds of individuals promote it? Different utilitarians answered this differently. Bentham relied largely upon self-interested actors guided by well-structured institutions to achieve greater aggregate happiness, because he had little expectation that people could improve. Mill, on the contrary, thought many of the ills of English society were due to a culture of self-interestedness, and he entertained, as we shall see, more robust hopes than Bentham for what humanity could become and for what kinds of happiness we could experience. Actualizing our potential in this regard depended, however, on receiving the right kinds of education. The intellectual's job is determining what kinds of education are the right ones.

Mill divides education into three varieties: intellectual, moral and aesthetic. Intellectual education covers cognitive development. Moral education, which occasionally overlaps with the aesthetic, promotes feelings of duty, i.e. the development of conscience. Aesthetic education is 'the education of the feelings, and the cultivation of the beautiful', which amounts to the development of dispositions of feeling and of imagination.[16] 'Aesthetic' here is employed ambiguously. It connotes both the means whereby one gets an aesthetic education, i.e. 'poetry and art', and the major goals of that education, namely the culture of specific feelings and of an aesthetic sensibility whose foundation is a developed imagination. Aesthetic education, however, is also broader than what might be suggested by the connection to art. As will become apparent, the cultivation of feeling and imagination relies just as much on institutional structures and habitual activities as it does on our experience of art.

Mill's inclusion of the aesthetic as a principal component of character development represents a break from the predominant tendencies in Victorian society (especially the evangelical ones) and reflects the influence of different strands of Romanticism and of German thought (as seen by Mill largely through the lens of British thinkers like Coleridge, Carlyle, Maurice and Sterling). By emphasizing aesthetic education, Mill aligns himself against what he took to be a kind of moral narrowness (e.g. 'the pinched and hidebound type of human character' that concerned itself almost exclusively with duty and conscience), and encourages the possibility of taking the human being as a 'noble and beautiful object of contemplation'.[17] In this respect, his ideas have interesting relations to the German notion of Bildung, which, as Collini describes it, 'suggests an openness to experience, a cultivation of the subjective response, an elevation of the aesthetic, and an exploratory attitude towards one's own individuality and potential.'[18]

Studying Mill's views on aesthetic education is attractive for a number of reasons. First, it transforms a wholly unwieldy subject, namely Mill's outlook on character development in general, into something a little less unwieldy, namely his position on the cultivation of feelings and imagination.

Second, the advantage of looking at education (as opposed to ideals of character abstracted from their genesis and the processes of maintenance) is that it consistently puts before our eyes the mechanisms whereby character ideals get promoted and sustained *over time*.[19] This allows us to identify more fully what is implied in living a Millian life – what commitment to such a life would mean for day-to-day practice – thereby enabling us to subject Mill's ideas to meaningful analysis and to think more clearly about whether, as an ethicist, Mill has continuing importance for us.

Third, Mill differentiates his ethical positions from those of Bentham and his father by emphasizing the need to attend to our affective and imaginative development. His portrayal of his own 'mental crisis' in the *Autobiography*, whether accurate or not, makes this clear. This point of tension with his teachers is also that point at which much of the influence of various critics of utilitarianism (e.g. Coleridge, Carlyle, Southey, Ruskin, Mackintosh, etc.) can be felt.[20] By examining this element of Mill's thought, we can get an improved sense of his relation to the intellectual milieu of his time.

Lastly, there has been very little work done directly on the subject of Millian aesthetic education, though there are writings on themes that run throughout this book.[21] Included among them are writings on the imagination,[22] art,[23] character[24] and religion.[25]

Analysing aesthetic education presents a number of difficulties, however. Mill does not devote a separate treatise to the topic, and the language he uses to talk about it can be imagistic and uninformative. One of the most important goals of this work, then, is to give an account of aesthetic education that makes it more amenable to appraisal. This requires an engagement with numerous debates in the period – debates about art, the importance of different feelings for ethical life, and the proper role of the moral imagination, for example. Mill's language is not detailed enough, his reliance on shared understanding with Victorian readers is too great, to forgo the requisite historical research.[26] If we want to grasp the content of his claims about aesthetic education, we need to see how those claims come out of, or are responses to, others made by the thinkers with whom Mill is familiar.

Since aesthetic education often 'comes through poetry and art' and involves the education of feelings and the cultivation of the beautiful, the book begins by examining Mill's views on poetry, art and the beautiful. Chapter 1 reconstructs Mill's positions on art criticism and on the nature of art and aesthetic experience with an eye to the ethical relevance of those positions. It shows how Mill characterizes poetry by contrasting it with rhetoric and the novel (or, more properly, the novelistic attitude), and how aesthetic experience or experience of the beautiful depends upon the capacity of the imagination to idealize the aesthetic object ('cultivation of the beautiful' in aesthetic education thus amounts to cultivation of specific imaginative capacities). This material acts as background for the book as a whole. The chapter ends by analysing the notion of 'life as art', that is, the idea that life itself is something to be conceived of using aesthetic categories, and by asking what could have motivated Mill to speak in these terms.

Chapter 2 examines the vague notion of the 'internal culture' of the affections, a primary desideratum of aesthetic education, and makes it more determinate through a contrast with Bentham's views on the cultivation of the feelings and a comparison with alternative positions articulated by critics of utilitarianism. How Mill acts to address three basic criticisms of Bentham's account provides us with a much clearer idea of what kinds of feeling and disposition good character development requires. Through this we attain new insight concerning Mill's perspectives on the place of character in ethical theory, on the higher pleasures, and on pleasures of sympathy.

Chapter 3 investigates the cultivation of the imagination by examining Mill's notion of the 'Religion of Humanity', in which he attempts to salvage the ethical benefits of religious belief while rejecting its metaphysical and moral baggage. Though the religious imagination traditionally supplied 'ideal conceptions grander and more beautiful than we see realized in the prose of human life' – conceptions that helped to mitigate the negative effects of the growth of industrial society – Mill thinks that an idealized humanity can substitute for a traditional God as an object of reverence and thereby serve the same ethical purpose.[27] Influenced by Comte, Mill wants to foster compelling narratives about an idealized humanity and an individual's relation to it. The chapter ends by indicating how Mill attempted to solve the problems raised by Bentham's attack on ethical employment of the imagination.

In the last two chapters, the focus switches from the character ideals fostered through aesthetic education to a more active engagement with important mechanisms of that education, thereby demonstrating the close relation of ethics to social and political reform. Beyond the experience of art, the mechanisms of aesthetic education also include institutions, particularly those of family and workplace. By examining what Mill has to say about how inequality in the family and opposition of interests in the workplace undermine the goals of aesthetic education, and how reform of those institutions can serve to further those goals, we get a vivid picture of a Millian life – not as a set of static ideals, but as a set of commitments, relationships and activities realized over time.

Lastly, the Conclusion looks back on the major themes examined in the study, with special attention given to the ways in which this book 're-thinks' Mill's ethics.

Mill has a great deal to say in reply to specific questions concerning the possibilities of human ethical development in the context of industrial modernity. This has not gone unnoticed, but it has gone without the articulation it deserves. His writings present and defend – sometimes clearly, sometimes disjointedly and haphazardly – different visions of admirable, detestable, regrettable and promising character. The hope is that by exploring this aspect of Mill's writings, his concrete ethical commitments will shine forth and inform our thinking about the challenges we face in ethical life, possible ways to address them, and what basis, if any, we have for optimism.

Endnotes

1. Arthur Schopenhauer, *On the Basis of Morality* (Indianapolis, IN: Hackett Publishing Company, 1995), 190.

2. Maurice Mandelbaum, *History, Man, and Reason: A Study in Nineteenth Century Thought* (Baltimore, MD: The Johns Hopkins Press, 1971), 196–7.

3. John Stuart Mill, *The Collected Works of John Stuart Mill*, gen. ed. John M. Robson, 33 vols (Toronto: University of Toronto Press, 1963–91), X:337.

4. Mill, *Collected Works*, X:219. This distinction is present in one of the earliest critical writings on Bentham's ethics. Sir James Mackintosh's *Dissertation Second: Exhibiting a General View of the Progress of Ethical Philosophy, Chiefly during the 17th and 18th Centuries*, which was prefixed to the seventh edition of the *Encyclopedia Britannica* (1830), contends that Bentham makes the mistake of assuming that 'because the principle of utility forms a necessary part of every moral theory, it ought therefore to be the chief motive of human conduct' (379).

5. Ronald Hamowy, *The Scottish Enlightenment and the Theory of Spontaneous Order* (Carbondale, KS: Southern Illinois University Press, 1987), argues that this basic idea had its first serious articulation in Mandeville.

6. Adam Smith, *An Inquiry into the Nature and Causes of the Wealth of Nations*, gen. eds. Cambell and Skinner, 2 vols (Indianapolis, IN: Liberty Press, 1981), I:456 [IV.ii.9], italics added.

7. Henry Home (Lord Kames), *Essays on the Principles of Morality and Natural Religion* (Indianapolis, IN: Liberty Fund, 2005), 46.

8. According to Halevy and others, Bentham could also be a source of this idea. Since, in Bentham's view, the dominant motive in human actions is self-interest, the way to further the general happiness is through directing individuals through sanctions, especially those established by legislation. The goal is not to get individuals to care about the general happiness. The goal is to have them promote it rather than hinder it as they pursue their own interests. This will be discussed in more detail in Chapter 2. See Elie Halevy, *The Growth of Philosophic Radicalism* (Boston, MA: Beacon Press, 1966).

9. For an expansive contemporary view that develops these ideas, see John Gray's account of Hayek: *Hayek on Liberty*, 3rd edn (London: Routledge, 1998), Ch. 2.

10. Mill, *Collected Works*, X:110–11.

11. Mill, *Collected Works*, X:181.

12. Mill, *Collected Works*, X:182.

13. Smart notes other reasons why utilitarians might rely on general rules rather than on the principle of utility when engaged in deliberation. Included among them are lack of time to work out the consequences resulting from

a particular choice and a tendency towards self-bias in calculating conse-quences. See J. J. C. Smart, 'Extreme and Restricted Utilitarianism', *The Philosophical Quarterly* (October 1956), 344–54.

14. Mill, *Collected Works*, XV:762.

15. J. O. Urmson, 'The Interpretation of the Moral Philosophy of J. S. Mill', *The Philosophical Quarterly* (January 1953), 33–9.

16. Mill, *Collected Works*, XXI:251.

17. Mill, *Collected Works*, XVIII:266.

18. Stefan Collini, 'The Idea of "Character" in Victorian Political Thought', *Transactions of the Royal Historical Society*, 5th series, 35 (1985), 29–50.

19. Knowledge of these mechanisms and, more broadly, of the causes of character are part of Mill's science of ethology.

20. Mandelbaum identifies two points of influence on Mill's thought of the 'Germano-Coleridgians', namely 'his recognition of the need for a concrete-historical rather than a psychological-deductive approach to history and government; and, second, his recognition of the fact that the views of human nature accepted by Bentham and his father placed too little emphasis on feelings and on the imagination'. Mandelbaum, *History, Man and Reason*, 194.

21. Works that do discuss or prominently mention aesthetic education include: Wendy Donner, *The Liberal Self: John Stuart Mill's Moral and Political Philosophy* (Ithaca, NY: Cornell University Press, 1991), Ch. 5; Maurice Mandelbaum, *History, Man and Reason*, Ch. 11; John M. Robson, *The Improvement of Mankind: The Social and Political Thought of John Stuart Mill* (Toronto: Toronto University Press, 1968); Alan Ryan, *The Philosophy of John Stuart Mill* (London: Macmillan, 1970), Ch. 13; F. Parvin Sharpless, *The Literary Criticism of John Stuart Mill* (The Hague: Mouton & Co., 1967); Susan Feagin, 'Mill and Edwards on the Higher Pleasures', *Philosophy* 58 (1983): 244–52; and Robert Scott Stewart, 'Mill's Theory of Imagination', *History of Philosophy Quarterly*, vol. 10, no. 4 (1993): 369–88.

22. See Feagin, and Stewart.

23. See Feagin, Sharpless and, most prominently, M. H. Abrams, *The Mirror and the Lamp: Romantic Theory and the Critical Tradition* (Oxford: Oxford University Press, 1953).

24. See Donner, Ryan, Mandelbaum and Janice Carlisle, *John Stuart Mill and the Writing of Character* (Athens, GA: University of Georgia, 1991).

25. James E. Crimmins, *Secular Utilitarianism: Social Science and the Critique of Religion in the Thought of Jeremy Bentham* (Oxford: Clarendon Press, 1990); Linda C. Raeder, *John Stuart Mill and the Religion of Humanity* (Columbia, MO: University of Missouri Press, 2002); Andrew Wernick, *Auguste Comte and the Religion of Humanity* (Cambridge: Cambridge University Press, 2001);

T. R. Wright, *The Religion of Humanity: The Impact of Comtean Positivism on Victorian Britain* (Cambridge: Cambridge University Press, 1986).

26. For all the value of Donner's book, and with recognition that her project is different, her treatment of aesthetic education is compromised by its exclusive dependence on Mill's texts, which themselves often tell us precious little. This is a common problem in the (strictly philosophical) secondary literature.

27. Mill, *Collected Works*, X:419.

1

The Ethics of Aesthetics and Life as Art

Why should we be interested in Mill's aesthetic theory? Though a moderately important representative of one school of criticism, he did not compose a major work on the subject, nor did he write with any great originality. His views on aesthetics, unlike his views on logic, ethics, economics, etc., were not terribly influential. Rather than the foundation of thinking in this subject, his writings are more like the roofing or interior design in a house built by someone else.

Though the intrinsic value of Mill's work in aesthetics is not particularly high (as he would acknowledge), his writings on literature and the fine arts represent an underexploited resource for understanding his ethical theory. It is a resource due to the close relationship of the aesthetic and ethical in his thought.

In the Victorian period, Mill is hardly unique in emphasizing the ties between aesthetics and ethics, but that tradition was not the only available possible stance towards the ethical status, if any, of art. Included among the early- to mid-century attitudes towards art were: 1) a deep suspicion of art by Puritans; 2) a burgeoning aestheticism that construed aesthetic experience as being about pleasure and that peaked in the latter part of the century with people like Pater and Wilde; 3) the idiosyncratic Benthamite concern for the social value of art as a source of pleasure and, potentially, prejudice (i.e. the unjustified use of 'taste' in judging a person's 'quality'); and 4) a moral tradition, best represented by Ruskin and including Mill, which argued for the ethical importance of art above and beyond any immediate pleasure it might provide.[1]

For Mill, art serves two basic types of ethical purpose. First, and most importantly, it acts to cultivate our feelings and imaginations, thereby fostering individuality. Second, beauty and the taste required to appreciate it embody ideals that are moral, not simply aesthetic, and that ultimately have a transformative effect on how we view our lives. This reflects the expansion of aesthetic categories and attitudes into the realm of the traditionally moral.

In the most general sense, art and aesthetic experience were taken as defending the integrity of the self by strengthening and articulating the 'inner' (including, as Mill would put it, our 'individuality'), so that it can resist the solvent effects and homogenizing tendencies of mass, industrial, democratic society. An investigation into his views on art is indispensable for understanding the nature and importance of aesthetic education, since the great moral interest in art and aesthetic experience consistently indicates an interest in our affective and imaginative well-being and development.

This chapter has two sections. In the first, I shall reconstruct Mill's aesthetic theory (in both earlier and later incarnations). Though I shall be trying to make the outlines of his views determinate, my interest is not in his theory per se, but in what that theory tells us about his ethical positions. This leads me to emphasize his accounts of 1) what distinguishes art (in the paradigmatic form of poetry) from other products and activities; 2) what constitutes engaging with something aesthetically; 3) the mechanisms that explain aesthetic experience; and 4) what makes a work of art or an observer of art good (thereby showing how the articulation of norms for art leads to the articulation of ethical norms). We will see how Mill links aesthetic experience to ideals of the imagination and to the cultivation of feeling and interiority.

In the second section, I shall examine what it means for Mill that the self becomes something to be treated aesthetically – how it should be thought of as a work of art and how we should come to view ourselves from an aesthetic point of view. The goal here is to move beyond vague, imagistic language in order to see what philosophical content we can give to the idea of life as art. I shall show how this represents a break from Bentham, what it says about Mill's 'perfectibilism', and how it expresses one of Mill's most basic anxieties about individuality in industrial modernity.

The harvest from these analyses will continue to be reaped in subsequent chapters when I shall discuss the specifics of the cultivation of imagination and feeling.

Mill's aesthetic theory

Early aesthetic theory

If the frequently cited influence of Romanticism on Mill is to have any purchase, it must surely be found in his aesthetics. Indeed, as Abrams notes, Mill's early theory of poetry relies heavily on Wordsworth's preface to the *Lyrical Ballads*.[2] Even if he lacks groundbreaking insights in aesthetics, Mill is nevertheless an important representative of the move from neo-classical aesthetic standards to Romantic ones.

His most thorough essay on the arts, 'Thoughts on Poetry and Its Varieties',[3] follows Wordsworth in arguing for an expressivist theory of poetry and other arts, which contends that the aesthetic value of art is constituted by the emotional self-expression of the artist, the overflow of which leads to the creation of the work. Mill begins to develop this theory by trying to characterize poetry (the paradigmatic art) through showing what it is not. Attention to the contrasts made with poetry will enable some preliminary comments about what makes something a work of art and what distinguishes the good from the bad art appreciator.

First of all, Mill accepts Wordsworth's opposition of poetry with science. The latter addresses itself to belief and operates through reason and rational persuasion. The former focuses on the emotions and operates through imagination and affective response. Science speaks a language attuned to the understanding, while poetry's language is attuned to the feelings. As Abrams notes in relation to Wordsworth, the traditional opposition of poetry to history, grounded on their differing objects of representation (i.e. poetry represents the universal and ideal, and history shows particular, actual events), is dropped in favour of the opposition of poetry to science, which grows out of the increased emphasis placed on the distinction of emotive/expressive versus cognitive/descriptive language.[4]

Interestingly, this parallels a change in poetry's closest artistic relations. From the Greeks to Mill's time, with Horace as the most famous representative of this tradition, poetry was frequently compared to painting. Both were, on the authority of Aristotle, paradigmatic realizations of the primary function of art – the imitation of nature.[5] The emphasis on imitating nature makes their similarities with science more obvious than any opposition.

Towards the end of the eighteenth century, however, in both England and Germany, a shifting conception of poetry moved it away from painting and the ideal of imitation, towards the expressive, and towards a perception of a closer relationship with that more abstract art, music.[6] The imitation of nature, always a somewhat hazy goal for art, was becoming problematized as the seeds of non-representational art took root. Under these influences, the shared features of poetry and music became more noticeable.[7]

The second opposition of poetry, and thus of art more generally, is made with the novel. Whereas poetry excites interest on the basis of its exploration of feeling, the novel depends upon interest aroused through incident or 'mere outward circumstances'.[8] Mill's use of 'mere' indicates the aesthetic superiority of the poem to the novel and, as we will see in a moment, that the lover of poetry possesses ethical advantages over the lover of the novel.[9] Not only is enjoyment of the first superior to enjoyment of the second, but the dispositions towards each type of enjoyment are rarely found together in one person. The conflict between poetic and novelistic natures is revealed by the fact that 'a really strong passion for either of the two, seems to presuppose or to superinduce a comparative indifference to the other'.[10]

Mill's favour for poetry over the novel, and for the poetic person over the novelistic person, comes out in the following important passage:

The sort of persons whom not merely in books but in their lives, we find perpetually engaged in hunting for excitement from without, are invariably those who do not possess, either in the vigor of their intellectual powers or in the depth of their sensibilities, that which would enable them to find ample excitement nearer at home. The same persons whose time is divided between sight-seeing, gossip, and fashionable dissipation, take a natural delight in fictitious narrative; the excitement it affords is of the kind which comes from without. Such persons are rarely lovers of poetry, though they may fancy themselves so, because they relish novels in verse. But poetry, which is the delineation of the deeper and more secret workings of the human heart, is interesting only to those to whom it recalls what they have felt, or whose imagination it stirs up to conceive what they could feel, or what they might have been able to feel, had their outward circumstances been different.[11]

A number of things need to be noted here. First of all, this characterization of the contrast of poetry with novels carries within it the familiar distinction of the descriptive from the narrative, which offers insight into Mill's conception of art and his ranking of its genres.[12] His antipathy for narrative in the arts takes the form of his general dislike of the genres of historical painting and of epic poetry.[13]

Second, and following up on the preceding point, this text exemplifies a continuing emphasis throughout Mill's aesthetic writings on the connection between art and the development of interiority. The development of interiority ('individuality' in the language of *On Liberty*) seems to mean a few things for him: 1) having a character which resists change in the face of shifting circumstance; 2) a capacity to find pleasure in solitude and in lingering over nature, art, and oneself; and 3) a resistance to the solvent effects of mass society (e.g. the pressures exerted by the tyranny of the majority). An inability to take an interest in the descriptive, that is, an excessive attachment to the external and public (which are the central elements of narrative), indicates ethical impoverishment. Though I cannot make a decisive argument for this at the moment (it will be addressed more fully in Chapter 2), this suggests two claims of Benthamite utilitarianism which Mill wants to revise: 1) in moral judgement, Bentham prioritizes the externality and publicity of action over internal character, largely due to his belief that there is no objective way to evaluate the worth of states of feeling apart from their tendency to produce consequences; and 2) Bentham's emphasis on legislation and jurisprudence places a great deal of weight on publicity against subjectivity. In other words, Mill's valorizing of poetry over the novel can be seen as indicative of his complaint that Bentham has overemphasized the centrality of action (rather than character and feeling) for morality.

A third point to draw from the passage above is that a capacity for turning within also entails the possibility of access to hidden features of human experience. Mill often utilizes 'depth' imagery in discussing human psychology to distance his position from what he considered to be the oversimplified Benthamite accounts, i.e. one should not ignore the 'deeper and more secret workings of the human heart' even in thought concerned only with action or legislation.[14]

Lastly, the imagination is featured prominently and in a way which presages the attractiveness of Ruskin's aesthetics for Mill. As we will see shortly, the peculiarly aesthetic activity of the imagination will receive greater articulation through Mill's engagement with Ruskin.

Another contrast for poetry is found in eloquence. Both are alike in being 'the expression or utterance of feeling', but rhetorical feeling remains concentrated on an audience while poetry is unselfconscious.[15]

The rhetorical tradition in aesthetics, in which the function of art lay in evoking some kind of reaction from audiences, has a long history. Generally, the reaction desired was emotive and/or educational, i.e. pleasure and/or instruction. The good artist, on this view, attends carefully to the relationship of the artwork and its observer, trying to shape the work in accordance with the psychological propensities of the spectator. The work of art, then, is the product of negotiation and compromise with the audience.

Poetry for Mill, alternatively, is 'feeling, confessing itself to itself in moments of solitude, and embodying itself in symbols, which are the nearest possible representations of the feeling in the exact shape in which it exists in the poet's mind'.[16] Oratory also depends on signs for the expression of feeling but the signs are employed purposefully for use in voluntary communication with others, while the poetic signs and symbols 'escape from us when we are unconscious of being seen'.[17] On this view, the distinctly aesthetic features of an artwork are, therefore, only contingently related to a spectator.

Mill heightens the contrast by suggesting that whereas rhetoric or eloquence is *heard*, poetry is *overheard*.[18] He means that the poet, unlike the rhetorician, is ideally unconcerned with audience. The poet is, for Mill, an essentially non-theatrical identity. One may have a flamboyant and highly performative personality and also be a poet, but one cannot be flamboyant and performative while writing genuine poetry. To encounter a good poem is to witness unselfconsciousness. Poetry is emotive expression for its own sake, rather than as an instrument employed to convince or move another. Whereas eloquence grows out of 'intercourse with the world', poetry is the 'natural fruit of solitude and meditation'.[19]

This distinction carries over into the passions expressed and evoked by the poetic and the rhetorical. The poetic deals with human feeling at its most natural, namely at its most private and earnest.[20] The poetic feeling is that absorbed in itself, where 'the mind is at least as much occupied by a passive state of its own feelings, as by the desire of attaining the premeditated end which the [rhetorical] discourse has in view'.[21] To lack the capacity for poetic feeling is an important sign of one's lack of humanity. The feelings reflected in and aroused by art, as we shall see later, are necessary for the development of character, particularly for character as understood in opposition to immersion in the social.

Given Mill's contrasts, what does a work of art as distinguished from works of science, novels and rhetoric, look like? As a somewhat trivial, but nonetheless helpful example of art, Mill offers a lion being described by the painter or poet. The lion as art should not be seen through the eyes of a scientist or naturalist, which should be guided by the search for truth, but through the eyes of the artist, which pick out those aspects of the lion that best express the feelings of the artist. As a naturalist, one examines the lion to understand it – its behaviour, biology, mechanical properties, etc. The lion as aesthetic, however, becomes a sign – it points to something beyond itself. If the artist has drawn or described it well, and if the appreciator has the requisite capacities for appreciation, the object acts on the imagination to indicate a state of mind. Thus the aspects of an object which are most properly aesthetic are those which best serve to signal the feelings of an observer, in contrast to those aspects which best serve science, i.e. those important in categorizing or in establishing causal laws. That ultimately means that the poet describes 'the lion professedly, but the state of excitement of the spectator really'.[22] The aesthetic aspects of something are those connected to human emotion, and for something to be good poetry, it must paint these emotions 'with scrupulous truth'.[23]

Objects taken aesthetically, that is, objects which are attended to on the basis of their aesthetic features, do not appear 'as they are' in their 'bare and natural lineaments', but rather as 'seen through the medium and arrayed in the colours of the imagination set in action by the feelings'.[24] Mill goes on to say that 'every truth which a human being can enunciate, every thought, even every outward impression, which can enter into his consciousness, may become poetry when shown through any impassioned medium, when invested with the colouring of joy, or grief, or pity, or affection, or admiration, or reverence, or awe, or even hatred or terror: and, unless so coloured, nothing, be it as interesting as may be, is poetry'.[25] The quality of one's aesthetic experiences depends very much on the type of 'impassioned medium' into which one can translate one's mental contents, and the 'state of excitement of the spectator' depends in turn on the nature of one's imagination and feelings.

Though there are some problems with the details, Mill's general intent is relatively clear. Aesthetic value rests in the manner in which an artist is able to capture, in whatever medium he uses, the expression of an emotion. As with the lion, so too with more complex subjects: the subject of the work is shown as it appears to one who is consumed by the feelings that the subject inspires, and the imaginative spectator is, through the help of the artist, moved towards a similar state of mind.

This reveals a central way that art aids in the cultivation of the feelings. The symbols and images of the artist, when felicitously chosen, act as catalysts for the observer of the artwork, such that even where a certain imaginative strength is lacking in the observer, the artist can facilitate the observer's affective responses. This deepens her emotional reserves and uncovers new possibilities for nuance in feeling.

This suggests that it is not only the poet who must understand introspection and separation from the bustle of everyday existence; the appreciator of poetry must as well. It is the turn inward leading to a more varied and authentically human emotional life which poetry depends upon and celebrates. Without having embraced this self-reflexivity, the reader of poetry will not be able to engage the poem. She will simply not understand the emotions that the poet ponders, because she will not have had them. The depth of the poet's emotions can only be plumbed by someone who has an adequate rope.

In Mill's early writings on poetry, therefore, the work of art expresses feeling. To encounter an object aesthetically is to do so emotively. The person who is capable of appreciating the work of art, then, is the one who engages it with the appropriate capacity for feeling and with a vigorous imagination. To confront the aesthetic aspects *as* aesthetic requires doing so as an affective, imaginative being, not as a cognizer (i.e. not primarily through the operation of reason on the senses). In addition, both the creation of art and the appreciation of it demand freedom from the distraction of social performance, that is, freedom from the complementary roles of rhetorician and audience member. One needs to be able to lose oneself in the exploration of feeling if one is to truly perceive what such feelings are like.

This general position leaves certain questions unanswered, however. First of all, Mill's understanding of what distinguishes the aesthetic experience seems too broad. He is committed to an account, a common-place in the period, in which the feeling associated with beauty is phenomenally distinct from other feelings.[26] And yet, many apparently non-aesthetic experiences involve the expression of feelings – what makes the genesis of our aesthetic experience unique? To put it another way, the uniqueness of aesthetic experience cannot be accounted for by appeal to the mere expression of feeling (even if we accept the distinction between rhetorical and poetic feeling). Certainly, a field of red paint on canvas could give me a non-theatrical joy in leading me to imagine eating a strawberry. Is that so clearly an aesthetic experience?

Mill's views also do not articulate well the similarity between our experiences of beauty in nature and in artworks. That a beautiful natural scene expresses an overflow of feeling by the artist is simply not prima facie credible, and Mill will want to be able to account for both kinds of beauty in similar ways.

To get some answers to these questions will require turning to Mill's more cursory later writings on aesthetic matters, in which he follows the lead of John Ruskin.

Ruskin

In the 1869 re-release of James Mill's *Analysis of the Phenomena of the Human Mind*, which the son edited and contributed notes to, we find a couple of pages of comment on his father's position on the experience of beauty. In this section, we learn that James Mill had the misfortune of having to rely on Archibald Alison for aesthetics, not having the benefit of referring to 'a deeper thinker than Alison', namely Ruskin. 'Mr. Ruskin, with profounder and more thoughtful views respecting the beauties both of Nature and of Art than any psychologist I could name, undertakes, in the second volume of *Modern Painters* [1846] to investigate the conditions of Beauty.'[27] Ruskin is, in Mill's judgement, 'to a very considerable degree successful in making out his case' concerning beauty, and, in particular, in distinguishing beauty from agreeableness. A reconstruction of Mill's aesthetic position benefits immensely from contextualization by Ruskin, because Mill depends upon Ruskin's greater acuity concerning the nature of beauty, and more importantly for our story, because Ruskin is the great mid-century champion of 'moralism' in art. Mill's agreement with Ruskin about beauty signals a deeper agreement concerning the moral impor-tance of aesthetic experience (though they differ on why such experience has moral significance). We are left, therefore, with the happy task of revisiting a masterpiece, both of prose and of criticism: *Modern Painters*.

We can appreciate Ruskin's moralization of art through the statement, in the second volume of *Modern Painters*, of his goal: 'It is to summon the moral energies of the nation to a forgotten duty, to display the use, force, and function of a great body of neglected sympathies and desires, and to elevate to its healthy and beneficial operation that art, which, being altogether addressed to them, rises or falls with their variableness of vigor,—now leading them with Tyrtaean fire, now singing them to sleep with baby murmurings.'[28] This great duty, cultivating sensitivity to beauty, ultimately amounts to furthering man's 'use and function', which is 'to be the witness of the glory of God, and to advance that glory by his reasonable obedience and resultant happiness'.[29] This permits us to comprehend the urgency behind Ruskin's claim that the study of art and nature 'is no recreation; it cannot be learned at spare moments, nor pursued when we have nothing better to do. It is no handiwork for drawing-room tables; no relief of the ennui of boudoirs; it must be understood and undertaken seriously or not at all.'[30] As these passages demonstrate, Ruskin always remains acutely aware of the connections between aesthetics and ethics. And though he places a more traditional theological emphasis on aesthetic experience than Mill would, even that – as will become apparent when we examine his views on the Religion of Humanity in Chapter 3 – is not as foreign to Mill in spirit as one might initially think.

Ruskin's project in this part of his multi-volume work is to catalogue the ideas of beauty (i.e. those ideas which are expressed by the aesthetic object and which are responsible for our experience of the beautiful), and to elucidate the workings and proper objects of the two central faculties for the creation and appreciation of art, namely the imagination and what he calls the 'theoretic faculty', which can be taken as approximating 'taste' and which will occupy more of our attention.[31]

The theoretic faculty 'is concerned with the moral perception and appreciation of ideas of beauty'.[32] Ruskin implores the reader not to think of the theoretic faculty as the aesthetic faculty, because he believes that 'aesthetic' connotes a mere operation of sense, and sense is not capable of producing the experience of beauty. For the experience of beauty is not found in mere sensual pleasure. It involves, first and foremost, the presence of the emotions which help make up the very idea of beauty, including joy, love of the object, and thankfulness and veneration towards the intelligence in which we perceive kindness – the kindness reflected in beautiful things. Beauty is not seen in the properties of objects alone, for beauty is not a straightforwardly physical feature, as colour and shape are. These properties must express some feature of the divine (i.e. an idea of beauty) for the experience to be one of true beauty.[33] They express them, however, only to the observer who is prepared to see them. Without the proper theoretic faculty, we might notice these properties of objects and even find them agreeable, but we will never see the beauty.

The ideas of beauty are not perceived intellectually either, because the emotions helping to constitute ideas of beauty are not obtainable by or resultant from the intellect's operation. Our perception of beauty, rather than being sensual or intellectual, is a moral perception, 'dependent on a pure, right, and open state of the heart, both for its truth and for its intensity'.[34] Ruskin goes on to say, qualifying himself, that although those without pure hearts can have 'naturally acute perceptions of the beautiful', they can never 'comprehend it, nor receive good from it, but make it a mere minister to their desires, and accompaniment and seasoning of lower sensual pleasures, until all their emotions take the same earthly stamp, and the sense of beauty sinks into the servant of lust'. The theoretic faculty, therefore, is primarily a moral faculty, and the pleasures of our experience of beauty are derived from 'those material sources which are agreeable to our moral nature in its purity and perfection'.[35] This emphasis on the moral informs, as one might expect, Ruskin's view of who can count as a good evaluator of beauty.

Before characterizing the good evaluator, however, we need to look at what these ideas of beauty, whose perception is essential to the experience of beauty, are. Ruskin suggests that, if we can be reasonably sure that the objects of our concern are producing the same sensations in different observers, we should be able to 'reason ... as well as feel ... out' the qualities of material objects 'which are calculated to give us this universal pleasure'.[36] This involves shearing off those qualities which make something accidentally or temporarily pleasant, until we are left with those things which beautiful objects have in common with one another, 'which we may then safely affirm to be the cause of its ultimate and true delightfulness'.[37] Note that the classification of these ideas supplies a want in Mill's earlier views, because it tells us more about what features of the object trigger an aesthetic experience.

Ruskin's analysis leads him to put forward two broad categories: typical and vital beauty. Typical beauty, so called because it typifies or expresses divine attributes, is a category covering some external qualities of bodies which are absolutely identical in all things in which they occur – stone, flower, beast, or man – whether in nature or as represented in artworks.[38] It is the beauty of 'mere material loveliness' as it gestures towards perfection.[39] Vital beauty is, alternatively, 'the appearance of felicitous fulfillment of function in living things, more especially of the joyful and right exertion of perfect life in man'.[40] Whereas typical beauty depends on lines and colours, the formal elements of the theoretic objects, vital beauty depends upon functions inherent in the organism.[41]

Ruskin admits that there are myriad ways in which, whether by arbitrary association or by 'typical resemblance', matter may 'remind us of moral perfections'.[42] Nevertheless, there appear to be a few modes which regularly manifest themselves, whereby this class of experiences of beauty may be explained. The varieties of typical beauty include those arising from the divine types of infinity, unity, repose, symmetry, purity and moderation.

To illustrate more concretely what Ruskin is talking about, we can begin with the experience connected to infinity, or the 'type of divine incomprehensibility'.[43] The paradigmatic cases of this experience generally arise from certain effects of light, particularly the light of 'the declining or breaking day' and the luminous backgrounds of certain paintings. Such a light is sought by the eye, and perceived with 'a deeper feeling of the beautiful … a deeper feeling, I say, not perhaps more acute, but having more of spiritual hope and longing, less of animal and present life'.[44] The effects of light here, then, suggest various ideas of infinity, i.e. of incomprehensibility, which inspire reverence. It is telling, and it certainly would have resonated with Mill, that Ruskin draws a contrast between animality, understood as focus on the immediate and everyday, and what one must assume is humanity, characterized by yearning and a reaching out to the divine. This is similar to distinctions between ordinariness (animality, machines) and the transcendent or dignified (humanity) that can be found again and again in Mill's ethical writing, and which are often paired, as we shall see, with the contrast between the experience of agreeableness and the experience of beauty.[45]

Symmetry, something frequently associated with beauty, is characterized by Ruskin as the type of divine justice that is understood as the opposition of equal quantities to each other (versus proportion, which is the connection of unequal quantities with each other, and which plays a central role in unity as an idea of beauty). Symmetry is only a mode of arrangement, and thus a necessary, but not a sufficient condition of beauty. There are, after all, numerous symmetrical and yet ugly things, including 'many Elizabethan ornaments'.[46] Where symmetry is absent, however, the effects of passion and violence are increased. These latter emotions, though they may be important in many things we value about art (its ability to provoke us, or its cathartic value), conflict with the experience of beauty. This is also apparent in the idea of repose, which is opposed to passion, change or laborious exertion. Beauty, among other things, is never violent, never unbalanced, and it almost never involves struggle.

Lastly, moderation, like symmetry, is not itself productive of beauty, but its want is destructive of all beauty. Similar to symmetry, its absence is reflected in violence or extravagance. Such lack gives rise to that which 'in colour we call glaring, in form inelegant, in motion ungraceful, in language coarse, in thought undisciplined, in all unchastened; which qualities are in everything most painful, because the signs of disobedient and irregular operation'.[47] This quotation, which also provides us with a nice list of the adjectives assignable to the ugly, reveals that a pleasing and important quality of beautiful objects is the expression of a kind of self-command, a government by law.

Typical beauty, of which I have given only some instances, is thus that in matter which expresses various divine or moral perfections, which are 'the inevitable stamp of his image on what he creates'.[48] These perfections are the perfections of a particular aspect or group of aspects of an object (e.g. infinity), or those of the relationships which hold among different aspects (e.g. symmetry).

Turning briefly to vital beauty, Ruskin summarizes it as follows: 'Throughout the whole of the organic creation every being in a perfect state exhibits certain appearances, or evidences, of happiness, and besides is in its nature, its desires, its modes of nourishment, habitation, and death, illustrative or expressive of certain moral dispositions or principles.'[49] Through our sympathy with the happiness of organic beings (happiness being understood as the discharge of its function, with the virtues appropriate to that function – not happiness in terms of mere flourishing or pleasure), we look upon those creatures as most lovely who are also most happy. In addition, vital beauty is detected in the moral lessons that a creature is meant to provide, allowing us to class them 'in orders of worthiness and beauty according to the rank and nature of that lesson'.[50] Vital beauty, even more than typical beauty, is therefore dependent upon a theologically-grounded view of nature and of creatures as designed – a position that has an interesting place in Mill's thought.

Though vital beauty may be a partial exception, it should be evident that Ruskin, along with Mill, does not find different conceptions of beauty in nature and in the fine arts. Insofar as art and nature were both seen as designed or potentially so – Ruskin and Mill were still pre-Darwinian in this respect – aesthetic appreciation did not take on a fundamentally different character when moved from natural to artistic objects.[51]

Now that we have a preliminary sense of what aspects of objects can be said to be responsible for their beauty, the question arises: What is it that makes one sensitive to beauty – that allows one, among other things, to fulfil this great duty of bearing witness to God's beneficence? First of all, the observer must 'above all things' possess earnestness and feeling.[52] Without these, one can never approach an artwork or a scene in nature and appreciate it properly. Lacking earnestness implies an inability to take the object of appreciation seriously enough. Either one will never be able to give it enough sustained attention, or the attention will be directed towards ends beyond the experience of the object (fighting off ennui, for example). A dearth of feeling, on the other hand, means a deadness and blindness to beauty. We cannot coolly and from an emotional distance evaluate the beauty of an object in the way we might perceive its physical properties. Without feeling, the world is empty of aesthetic value. Feeling makes aesthetic perception possible.[53] If the emotions mentioned earlier that characterize the operations of the theoretic faculty are absent, we are only able to experience the merely animal pleasure of sensibility. The cultivation of an aesthetic sensibility, therefore, involves the cultivation of capacities for feeling.

In addition to being earnest and primarily affective, true taste, according to Ruskin, is always capable of being astonished. It is open to beauty in all its forms, wherever they may be: back alley, rustic field or art collection. The purity of our taste is testable by this universality, i.e.

by its ability to find beauty wherever it may look. True taste does not heed social distinctions or common opinion. False taste, on the other hand, is fastidious, full of pride and condescension, and remains far too aware of its own operation (presumably because it is aware of its being evaluated by others). It is theatrical, that is, it performs for others in what we could call a 'rhetorical mode', and thus generally fails to evaluate rightly, not being in the right spirit. False taste often misses much that would be worthy of it. The continuity of these views with Mill's earlier writings – the emphasis on sincerity, on quiet, earnest contemplation, on freedom from attitudes of social performance – is noticeable.

Another social danger to true taste is the problematic influence of custom, which can reconcile human nature 'to many things naturally painful to it, and even improper for it'.[54] Though the cultivation of our judgement must begin by depending on authority to tell us what is good and bad, custom and authority must ultimately give way to 'openness of heart, which proves all things'.[55]

Ruskin, then, does three things which are of special import for us, all of which reveal how closely tied the aesthetic is to the ethical. First of all, he articulates and emphasizes the central connection of beauty to perfection. Our experience of beauty is best understood as being constituted by our engagement with the perfection expressed, more or less opaquely, in aesthetic objects. This will be fundamental for comprehending the meaning of the aesthetic point of view in Mill's thought. Secondly, Ruskin's portrait of the good aesthetician reinforces the anti-rhetoric strand of Mill's earlier theory, while expanding it to include the observer of art as well, not just the artwork and the artist. The earnestness, purity, and depth of feeling in the person of true taste are understood through contrast to social performance. Concern about taste involves a concern about how much one's aesthetic judgement is constituted by specifically social influences. The role of aesthetician, just like that of poet or painter, is best characterized through a relation to a work of art or to a natural scene, not through a relation to other people. Lastly, Ruskin's language shows that the process of forming one's taste is a central task in the formation of one's soul. Becoming a good person is inseparable from developing one's taste for beauty.

Later Aesthetic Theory

Though Mill objected to some of the theological/metaphysical components of Ruskin's theory, he thought that the mechanics of it (e.g. the ideas
of beauty), reinterpreted through the psychological theory of associationism, were fundamentally correct. Moreover, the moralization of art
that Ruskin represents resonates with Mill's own attitudes. All of this
gives us an opportunity to render Mill's later aesthetic views with a bit
more sharpness than would have been possible had we simply focused on
his theories of poetry.

A basic contention in aesthetics of this time is that there is a phenomenological difference between the pleasure one gets in aesthetic
experience and other sorts of pleasures.[56] The central problem in aesthetic
analysis (one solved for Ruskin by appeal to ideas of beauty), is giving an
account of what causes the feelings which arise from aesthetic experience
to be different from those that originate in other types of experience,
particularly in the experience of the agreeable.

As an example of an aesthetic encounter, Mill offers a screen of trees
in windy country. Though Mill is not wholly explicit on this point, there
seem to be three ways in which the trees may produce pleasure. The first
would be through the sensation itself, anterior to association. The colours
of the trees, a deep green or brown, would be one possible instance. Mill
recalls 'the intense and mysterious delight which in early childhood I had
in the colours of certain flowers; a delight far exceeding any I am now
capable of receiving from colour of any description, with all its acquired
associations'.[57] There is a 'direct element of physical pleasure' which
associations simply do not give, and yet which is potentially available
in our encounter with the trees. It is also no accident that this form of
pleasure – one emphasized by aestheticism – is most closely linked to
childhood, where our emotive and cognitive lives are much less nuanced
and much less constituted by the accretions of association that build up
over time. This direct sensual experience depends almost entirely on
openness, on the absence of the cognitive and emotive friction exerted by
adults on most of their sensory input.

His brief discussion of music makes a similar point. Mill disagrees with
his father's contention that all the power that music and the human voice
have to please derives from the associations connected with them, and
asserts the following: 'That very much of the pleasure afforded by Music
is the effect of its expression, i.e. of the associations connected with sound,

most people will admit: but it can scarcely be doubted that there is also an element of direct physical and sensual pleasure.'[58] He goes on to argue that single sounds, harmony or lack thereof, and various melodies can be, in themselves, agreeable or disagreeable. 'With these pleasures those of the associated ideas and feelings are intimately blended, but may, to a certain extent, be discriminated by a critical ear. It is possible to say', he goes on, 'of different composers, that one (as Beethoven) excels most in that part of the effect of music which depends on expression, and another (as Mozart) in the physical part.'[59]

A second form of pleasure that the trees can provide is the pleasure of agreeableness. One example of this is the pleasure resulting from an association of the screen of trees with ideas such as warmth, comfort, and shelter – those things involved in pleasurably getting us through everyday life, and those things, concurring with Ruskin, more associated with our animality. As Mill argues, the state of consciousness made up of the associations of commonplace and everyday pleasures will not have as elevated a character as a state 'made up of reminiscences of such ideas as Mr. Ruskin specifies, and of the grand and interesting objects and thoughts connected with ideas like those'.[60] The former state of consciousness demands no particularly rare or deep affective capacity to enjoy. We are all familiar with the simple pleasures. In pleasures of agreeableness, those aspects of the trees that an observer attends to are those which lend themselves to a particular sort of imagining. We make present to ourselves the situation of comfort, and the pleasant feelings we experience result from our imagining the feelings that such situations provide.

The last way of perceiving such trees pleasurably is in relation to their beauty. Those elements of the trees which constitute its beauty 'appeal to other, and what we are accustomed, not without meaning, to call higher, parts of our nature; which give a stronger stimulus and a deeper delight to the imagination, because the ideas they call up are such as in themselves act on the imagination with greater force'.[61] Here, then, Mill draws on Ruskin's ideas of beauty, particularly the notion of typical beauty. He suggests that our awareness, though often 'vague and confused', of the ideas of beauty (infinity, symmetry, unity, etc.) is required for aesthetic perception.

But what is so special about this type of idea rather than others? Why couldn't other ideas serve the same purpose? The answer to this is relatively straightforward. With the special exception of infinity, which, by suggesting power or magnitude without limit, 'acquires an otherwise strange impressiveness to the feelings and imagination', the ideas of beauty 'all represent to us some valuable or delightful attribute, in a completeness and perfection of which our experience presents us with no example, and which therefore stimulates the active power of the imagination to rise above known reality, into a more attractive or a more majestic world'.[62] This will generally mean that we see or feel, more or less vaguely, the objects evoking these ideas as expressing aspects of human or natural perfection.[63] Our imaginative encounter with these perfections produces the pleasures considered distinctly aesthetic.

'Lower pleasures', on the contrary, including pleasures of agreeableness, do not stimulate the imagination 'to rise above known reality':

> To them there is a fixed limit at which they stop: or if, in any particular case, they do acquire, by association, a power of stirring up ideas greater than themselves, and stimulate the imagination to enlarge its conceptions to the dimensions of those ideas, we then feel that the lower pleasure has, exceptionally, risen into the region of the aesthetic, and has superadded to itself an element of pleasure or a character and quality not belonging to its own nature.[64]

A lower pleasure, like those tied to the sensation of rich colours, the harmonies of a Mozart piano concerto or the comfort implied by a screen of trees, does not provoke us beyond our 'known reality', and cannot do so without the aid of certain associated ideas of the sort that Ruskin reveals. If a particular object does not conduce to the production of these ideas, which might be said to act as our points of access to other imaginative horizons, then the pleasure will not be an aesthetic one.[65] Mill has, therefore, with Ruskin's help, identified more clearly than he had in his earlier works on poetry and art what generates the uniqueness of the aesthetic experience.

The ideas of beauty give Mill an arguably more robust set of conceptual resources through which he can characterize what marks out aspects of an object as potentially aesthetic. Whereas in his earlier writings he determines that the characteristic of the artwork is its expression of feeling through images that are amenable to it, here, by drawing on Ruskin's account, he gives a richer story of what we can expect these images and symbols that evoke the imagination to be like. Moreover, by focusing on the ideas of beauty, he is provided with a more palatable theory of what makes the aesthetic experience of beauty in nature similar to that in art. Beauties in nature and in art are not the expressions of emotions per se – this would make little sense for nature – they are the expressions of different kinds of perfections and qualities that provoke the imagination to vigorous activity, thus producing those 'imposing' feelings typical of beauty.[66] These emotions, in turn, act to signal the presence of beauty.

We might integrate Mill's earlier view with his later one if the artist's state of mind could be seen, albeit loosely, as itself embodying a perfection or an idea of beauty. The artist, in other words, attempts to bring the expression of a particularly striking (ideal) example of an emotion into whatever artistic medium he uses. Whether this synthesis gets off the ground or not, it should be clear that the centre of gravity in Mill's aesthetics has shifted to the notion of perfection and that the imagination possesses an even bigger role than previously.

We should now be able to give a preliminary answer to the question 'What does it mean to perceive something aesthetically?'. For Mill, imagination grounds aesthetic perception. We identify specifically aesthetic imagining by starting with those feelings and experiences which are distinctly aesthetic and giving an analysis of their genesis in the imagination. Such an analysis reveals that aesthetic imaginative activity, as opposed to the imagination's activity in mere daydreaming, in the pleasures of agreeableness, or in sympathy, is characterized by sensitivity to perfections of various kinds (i.e. ideas of beauty) embodied in features of aesthetic objects, which provoke the imagination into a 'more majestic world'. Such activity is made possible only through a specific orientation to observing – an orientation that is given content by its opposition to social performance. The good aesthetic observer is reflective, earnest and, like the artist, engaged in soliloquy.

This analysis of Mill's views on beauty indicates that the experience of beauty takes us outside of ordinary life, connecting us to ideals that anchor us in the face of the threats presented to individuality by urban, industrial modernity. For Mill, the culture of the individual – our ennoblement – depends upon our 'rising above known reality', because reality as it exists is not a good medium for cultivating our humanity. On this view, then, art is not pursued for its own sake – it carries ethical freight. Mill would concur with Ruskin's claim that 'you must not follow

Art without pleasure, nor must you follow it for the sake of pleasure'.[67] The latter phrase firmly rejects a basic tenet of aestheticism and situates the purposes of art in the realm of ethics.

Life as art

Alan Ryan ends *The Philosophy of John Stuart Mill* with the following sentences:

> And, however much at odds it sometimes is with his determinist universe, Mill's concern with self-development and moral progress is a strand in his philosophy to which almost everything else is subordinate. And this is why, once we have established the rational society, scientifically understood, controlled according to utilitarian principles, the goals we aim at transcend these, and can only be described as the freely pursued life of personal nobility – the establishment of the life of the individual as a work of art.[68]

Ryan's mention of life as art is not an arbitrary imposition onto Mill, who consistently uses aesthetic categories in treating the self and character. This is strikingly exemplified in the 'Inaugural Address Delivered to the University of St. Andrews' (1867) where the connection of art with life and character is made explicit: 'Art, when really cultivated, and not merely practised empirically, maintains, what it first gave the conception of, an ideal Beauty, to be eternally aimed at, though surpassing what can be actually attained; and by this idea it trains us never to be completely satisfied with imperfection in what we ourselves do and are: to idealize, as much as possible, every work we do, and most of all, our own characters and lives.'[69]

Another, and better-known example of the tendency to speak of life in relation to art comes from Chapter Three in *On Liberty*, where Mill claims that: 'It really is of importance, not only what men do, but also what manner of men they are that do it. Among the works of man, which human life is rightly employed in perfecting and beautifying, the first in importance surely is man himself.'[70]

Why does Mill present life in aesthetic terms, and what kind of philosophical content does this have? In this section, I will suggest two basic responses to these questions. First, life as art has clear ties, as we see from the preceding quotes, to striving for perfection. Though an often-noted element of Mill's ethical thought, his 'perfectibilism' receives additional helpful context by reference to his aesthetic writings. Second, Mill's use of 'life as art' expresses basic anxieties shared by numerous nineteenth-century British and Continental intellectuals about the loss of self threatened by industrial modernity. The ideal of the individual as artist of her own life (i.e. a self-maker) gives us another way to think about Mill's more famous notion of individuality.

Perfection

It should not surprise us given the discussion of Ruskin's influence on Mill that Mill consistently associates art with striving for perfection. Art is defined as 'the endeavour after perfection in execution'.[71] No other human productions 'come so near to perfection as works of pure Art' because 'perfection is itself the object' of artistic activity.[72]

Life as art, then, is life as viewed from the standpoint of perfectibility. At the most basic level, this implies the possibility of indefinite progress in the quality of our 'feelings and opinions'.[73] What form this progress is meant to take remains opaque. The following chapters will clarify the ideals which guide this progress and the means employed for achieving them. At present, it will be enough to note that aesthetic education builds sensitivity to perfection, and to notice possible analogies between the way in which the artist and the life-artist pursue perfection, that is, analogies between the invocation of perfection in aesthetics and ethics.

The first point can be dispatched rather quickly. Aesthetic education prods us to sensitivity to perfection and, in particular, sensitivity to its absence. We come to see our lives from an aesthetic point of view when we 'feel ... the absence of noble aims and endeavours, as not merely blameable but also degrading'.[74] This sensitivity to perfection 'which would make us demand from every creation of man the very utmost that it ought to give, and render us intolerant of the smallest fault in ourselves or in anything we do, is one of the results of Art cultivation'.[75] Sensitivity to perfection, after all, is what most aesthetic experience amounts to for Ruskin and for Mill, and it is what we learn – what we are guided to – by the great artist.[76]

Understanding the analogy between the artist's and life-artist's pursuit of perfection is more involved. Striving for perfection implies that it is not what the work produces (i.e. whether it is a painting, sculpture or a table) but the manner in which the work is done that characterizes the artist and differentiates him/her from the labourer. To make this point, Mill offers the example of a craftsman. Whether he strives after perfection (whether, that is, he is an artist) shows itself in the final product, which must bear the marks of being done as if the craftsman 'loved it, and tried to make it as good as possible, though something less good would have answered the purpose for which it was ostensibly made'.[77]

To get more concrete, think of the example of a table that a furniture maker is producing. The craftsman as artist tries to make the table better than it would need to be for the purposes it serves. For the table to be a product of artistic activity, the craftsman must have attended to it lovingly, being driven more by the logic of the activity rather than by the consequences of finishing (e.g. selling the table for a good price). That is, the artist will often spend hours on things that the normal user of the table might never really notice or come across, because the form or nature of this particular table seems to demand it. This may involve, for example, 'listening' to the demands made by the particular pieces of wood themselves, and letting them, to an extent, dictate the form of the final product. The table, then, must reflect a maker for whom the physical product and the activity of making it have intrinsic worth.

The artist who sees the intrinsic worth of the activity of making can be contrasted with those who sell tables to make a living *and* for whom the activity of table-making is dominated by that end. For such a person, the making of the table is not an artistic pursuit; it is merely instrumental to getting money. In such a case, the standards of what counts as good or bad table-making derive largely from what will sell and not from the standards intrinsic to the activity.

For the artist, however, the activity, while it is engaged in, is done for the sake of doing it (the artist can take into account what will sell, but cannot consistently instrumentalize the activity and still remain an artist). The artist attends to those things necessary to excellence in table-making, things that are most often learned by watching good craftspeople work and by working along with them. Fundamentally, this means that the artist occupies a different point of view from the workman, namely the point of view in which the activity and the thing being worked on are looked at with attention to how they can be made perfect according to standards internal to the activity. Striving for excellence means having a general disregard, at the time of the making, for the consequences that arise after the activity is completed, e.g. whether the table will sell or not.[78]

As we will see in Chapter 5, this characterization of the artist's work and Mill's commitment to the desirability of striving for perfection combine to induce him to make radical proposals for reform of the workplace.[79] Mill wants to take work beyond mere temporal concerns and into the realm of the spiritual.

What, then, does this tell us about the applicability of artistic sensibility to ethical concerns? Mill's views on aesthetics, including his emphasis on perfection and on the contrast of art with the novelistic and rhetorical spirits, reveal a manner of perceiving, evaluating, and shaping ourselves that infuses his ethical views. Life is not something merely to be lived and enjoyed (as Bentham thinks), but is capable of different kinds of perfection. An unwillingness to pursue perfection in our characters as the artist does in the artwork implies that our lives are being determined by goals and forces outside ourselves – that we are consumed by the novelistic bustle of life and by the non-idealized (rhetorical) audience to whose demands we submit ourselves.

This dovetails nicely, of course, with *On Liberty*, and provides another way of looking at the famous notion of individuality. The genuine individual is the life artist. He is able to turn his attention to shaping himself according to demands that he takes to be intrinsic to that activity, rather than demands placed upon him by the majority.

It also brings out the apparent influence on Mill of German thought and its emphasis on self-culture. Unfortunately for Mill, the spirit of perfection shows itself to be in uneasy alliance with the hedonism which he inherited, as we can see in this passage from the 'savant' Humboldt:

[States] desire comfort, ease, tranquility; and these are most readily secured to the extent that there is no clash of individualities. But what man does and must have in view is something quite different—it is variety and activity. Only these develop the many-sided and vigorous character; and, there can be no one, surely, so far degraded as to prefer, for himself personally, comfort and enjoyment to greatness; and he who draws conclusions for such a preference in the case of others may justly be suspected of misunderstanding human nature, and of wishing to make men into machines.[80]

On this view, perfection cannot simply be seen as a part of happiness. The two ends are different, and at times not compatible.

Bentham and Mill are invested heavily in an Epicurean reduction of all goods to happiness, so that practical life can have a common standard of value. This common standard is necessary, according to their view, if moral disagreement is to be rationally, rather than arbitrarily, resolved. Now, Mill's emphasis on beauty is, in part, an emphasis on perfection. As we have seen, however, and as many Germans knew well, it is not obvious that perfection and happiness can be easily allied and united. It could be that one must choose between them. To address this problem, Mill adopts qualitative distinctions among pleasures. Whether or not this succeeds, his motivations for doing so are clearer when placed in the context of discussion of life as art.

Anxieties about industrial modernity

If one were to look for what most clearly distinguishes Bentham from Mill, one could do far worse than to focus on anxiety. Bentham appears to lack it entirely. His writing often communicates passion, a hatred for injustice, and a hope for better governance, but never any hint of anxiety. Mill's work, on the other hand, is awash in it. This is what connects him most closely to Coleridge and Carlyle, and perhaps to the more general spirit of his age.

The propensity to speak of life in terms of art – to recommend viewing it as something to be perfected – indicates, I would suggest, anxieties about industrial modernity and a belief that art has an important role in treating the maladies of modernity. Though these anxieties will be canvassed much more extensively in the succeeding chapters, we can note some things here, particularly with reference to how the artistic sensibility is meant to protect the individual from the solvent of modern social life.

A pertinent example of Mill's concern for mass society can be found in *The Subjection of Women*.[81] In arguing for the desirability of an ideal of marriage in which mutual respect and admiration serve as the distinguishing marks, Mill suggests that the man who desires 'to attain exalted virtue', and 'to be better than public opinion requires him to be' will find a wife his inferior in intelligence 'a perpetual dead weight, or, worse than a dead weight, a drag' because the wife will be the 'auxiliary of the common public opinion'.[82] She will strive for 'consideration' instead of perfection. A man with children and such a wife 'has given hostages to Mrs. Grundy'.[83]

What is the contrast between consideration and perfection? Here, we are able to get more specific about what it actually means to attend to aspects of ourselves which can be treated aesthetically by the imagination versus those which cannot. Consideration and perfection essentially recapitulate in ethical life the contrast between agreeableness and beauty in aesthetics. Just as ideas like comfort, warmth, rest and shelter ground the pleasures of agreeableness, so similarly the wife concerned with consideration calls her husband's attention to those features of himself valued by society and for successfully navigating the course of quotidian existence, namely whether his political views are distasteful to others, if he 'has the reputation of mingling in low radical politics', if he obtains the invitations and honours that others do, if he has done something which 'hinders George [their son] from getting a commission or a place', or which prevents 'Caroline [their daughter] from making an advantageous match'.[84] She offers little support or encouragement when his desire to be virtuous, or his desire to endeavour after perfection, jeopardizes the 'sole return' that society makes to her for a life of 'continued self-sacrifice'. Eventually, he may no longer even be able to see himself aesthetic-ally, having been reduced to that 'mediocrity of respectability which is becoming a marked characteristic of modern times'. He will shape himself rhetorically rather than artistically, i.e. with special attention to his audience, which dispenses the consideration that he has come to value so much.[85]

Perfection, then, captures the imagination in a very different way from consideration. It is associated with those ideal conceptions of character and action (e.g. the gentleness and kindness of Christ, the wisdom and self-control of Socrates, the almost frightening sense of justice in Brutus, etc.) which are exemplified in various histories, religious texts, bio-graphies, poems, novels and dramas. The imagination is struck by the ease with which these figures lead it to a 'more majestic world', one which brings out, as does our experience of the beautiful, the exhilarating pos-sibilities latent in our humanity – possibilities not found when we dwell upon consideration, i.e. social acceptance, material success, etc. These possibilities seem to be, I would suggest, the virtues characteristic of those qualities 'which are the distinctive endowment of a human being', including judgement, discriminative feeling, mental activity, expansive sympathy, moral preference and, most importantly, the capacity of choice.[86] The person trying to be an artist of her own life must emulate the perfections of these capacities found in the great figures of history and literature, but always with an attention to her particularity, that is, to what possibilities of greatness are ready to be expressed by her own individual nature. With the right kind of aesthetic sensibility, fostered by an appropriately robust aesthetic education, she will avoid degradation and wallowing in animality, because she will be aware of the absence of grandeur and nobility in the picture that her life presents.[87] Moreover, if her intellectual education has kept apace, there will be no collapse into a sentimentalism that jeopardizes morality (morality depending, of course, on our clear-sighted, rational estimation of consequences and on our acceptance of the connected duties).[88]

The self taken from an aesthetic point of view – life as art – can thus be understood as helping to demarcate a realm of authenticity in opposition to the superficiality of mass society. Whereas social life exerts constant pressure towards uniformity, towards that efficiency of communication and transaction which arises from settled expectation about the behaviour and attitudes of others, authenticity depends on individuality, on norms that are not necessarily congruent with the norms that make social life function well. For Mill, we are only a genuine self – we only have a genuine character – insofar as we differentiate this self from unconscious unity with society. Vital to this process is the emergence of our intellectual capacities, whose dissolving powers help free us from being 'the dupe of every superficial appearance'.[89] But equally important is that attunement to our nature characterized by the aesthetic activity of the imagination. This means seeing ourselves as works of art, with all that implies, rather than primarily as incorporated into a social world.

Conclusion

This chapter serves three basic purposes. It works out the mechanisms of aesthetic experience as Mill portrays them, which will be very important when we discuss the details of aesthetic education. It shows how art becomes characterized and distinguished from other things. And lastly, it begins the process (which will be carried on in subsequent chapters) of showing what we can learn about Mill's ethical views by attention to his aesthetics, while revealing the anxieties that prompt him to characterize ethical life in aesthetic terms.

Endnotes

1. I am indebted to Nicholas Shrimpton's 'Ruskin and the Aesthetes' [in *Ruskin and the Dawn of the Modern*, ed. Dinah Birch (Oxford: Oxford University Press, 1999)] for the tripartite division of the artistic theoretical landscape of mid-century Britain into 'Puritanical, Theoretic [Ruskinian], and Aesthetic'. The addition of the fourth category (the Benthamite view) is justified in any study of Mill.

2. M. H. Abrams, *The Mirror and the Lamp: Romantic Theory and the Critical Tradition* (Oxford University Press, 1953).

3. John Stuart Mill, *The Collected Works of John Stuart Mill*, gen. ed. John M. Robson, 33 vols (Toronto: University of Toronto Press, 1963–91), I:343–65. It should be noted that this essay appears originally in the first edition of *Dissertations and Discussions* (1859), combining, with very little alteration, two earlier essays from 1833, 'What is Poetry?' and 'The Two Kinds of Poetry'.

4. Abrams, *The Mirror and the Lamp*, 101.

5. For a provocative account of the development of the mimetic conception of the arts among the Greeks, and of its ties to dramatic narrative, see E. H. Gombrich, *Art and Illusion* (Princeton: Princeton University Press, 1961), Chapter IV.

6. Abrams, *The Mirror and the Lamp*, 84. As an example of the move of poetry away from painting, see Lessing's *Laocoon*.

7. These shifts were mirrored in the changing fortunes of the various poetic forms. In the imitative critical tradition, the epic was the favoured genre. Among other things, it seemed to offer the appropriate space and structure for truthful imitation. The lyric, on the other hand, was frequently dismissed as superficial and trite, even if it was often pleasing. Within the expressivist critical tradition, however, the lyric dominated. Its relative brevity was considered perfectly suited for the main task of poetry: the expression of an emotive unity, i.e. of a simple and discernable feeling. Mill went so far as to voice the 'heretical' opinion that, except under special circumstances, 'a long poem will always be felt ... to be something unnatural and hollow', primarily because the advantages that rhythmic verse has in expressing 'deep and sustained feeling' are lost in more expansive poetic forms (see 'Writings of Alfred de Vigny' in Mill, *Collected Works*, I:498–9).

8. Mill, *Collected Works*, I:345. It should be noted that this is not an argument

for hierarchy of genres; it is a distinction between the main sources of interest in a work. That is, novels can be poetic, just as poems can be novelistic.

9. 'Novel-reader' tended to be a gendered category in Mill's Britain. Laments about the effects of novels on young women were common, and became particularly pressing with the rise of the Gothic novel of the late eighteenth and early nineteenth centuries.

10. Mill, *Collected Works*, I:345.

11. Ibid.

12. For helpful articles on narrative, with particular focus on the relation to description, see Svetlana Alpers, 'Describe or Narrate? A Problem in Realistic Representation', *New Literary History 8*, #1, Autumn 1976, 15–41; Gerard Genette, 'Boundaries of Narrative', *New Literary History 8*, #1, Autumn 1976, 1–13; A. R. Louch, 'Criticism and Theory', *New Literary History 8*, #1, Autumn 1976, 171–82. Mill's suspicion of narrative is undoubtedly influenced by Carlyle who labels it a 'mere chronicle of "occurrences"' ('On History Again' (1833) in Thomas Carlyle, *Critical and Miscellaneous Essays* (Philadelphia: Casey and Hart, 1845), 423). For both, such a chronicle does very little to illuminate the people involved in these occurrences.

13. Mill, *Collected Works*, I:352. In order to better understand the contrast of narration and description in art, it is helpful to compare Renaissance painting. As Alpers argues ('Describe or Narrate', 17, 24), Renaissance representation was dominated by the concern with narrative, because it was through narrative action that many Renaissance artists and thinkers believed painting was able to communicate truth about human beings. Without narrative action, a painting was felt to be largely devoid of meaning (thus the frequent denigration of the Dutch painters by those who felt that their work lacked interest). With Rembrandt, we find a move away from narration towards portrayal. Alpers contends that 'Psychological depth is suggested by a new kind of pictorial depth. Insofar, then, as Rembrandt trusts to the representational power of art, he is redefining what it is to represent, suggesting things that lie beneath the surface ... he is suggesting that this in-depth portrayal must replace narration as the expression of serious human interest' (24). Mill is a great admirer of Rembrandt and suspicious of history painting; he is an heir to the descriptive tradition in art. This tradition focuses more on contemplation rather than action, and on psychology over event.

14. As an example of this tendency see Mill, *Collected Works*, X:56; and X:97–8.

15. Mill, *Collected Works*, I:348.

16. Ibid., I:348–9.

17. Ibid., I:352.

18. Ibid., I:348.

19. Ibid., I:349.

20. Diderot makes a very similar point: 'It is rare that a being who is not totally engrossed in his action is not mannered. Every personage who seems to tell you: "Look how well I cry, how well I become angry, how well I implore," is false and mannered.' (Michael Fried, *Absorption and Theatricality: Painting and Beholder in the Age of Diderot* (Berkeley, CA: University of California Press, 1980), 99.)

21. Mill, *Collected Works*, I:362.

22. Ibid., I:347.

23. Ibid.

24. Ibid.

25. Ibid., I:348.

26. Though Mill was aware of other aesthetic categories, most obviously the sublime, he commonly fails to distinguish between the general aesthetic value of something and its beauty. I will continue this looseness here as I do not think it jeopardizes any of my arguments.

27. John Stuart Mill in James Mill, *An Analysis of the Phenomena of the Human Mind*, 2 vols, ed. John Stuart Mill (London: Longmans, Green and Dyer, 1869), II:252–3. Mill had a very high opinion of Ruskin as one can see in his diary entry for 21 January 1854: 'It is long since there has been an age of which it could be said, as truly as of this, that nearly all the writers, even the good ones, were but commentators: expanders and appliers of ideas borrowed from others. Among those of the present time I can think only of two (now that Carlyle has written himself out, and become a mere commentator on himself) who seem to draw what they say from a source within themselves: and to the practical doctrines and tendencies of both these, there are the gravest objections. Comte, on the Continent; in England (ourselves excepted) I can only think of Ruskin.' (Mill, *Collected Works*, XXVII:645.)

28. John Ruskin, *Modern Painters, Vol. II* (New York: D.D. Merrill Company, 1893), 3.

29. Ruskin, *Modern Painters, Vol. II*, 4.

30. Ibid., 2. Holger Hoock notes that in the 1830s a 'perceived political, moral, and cultural crisis intensified the connections made in public discourse between reform in the worlds of politics and art' ('Reforming culture: national art institutions in the age of reform', in *Rethinking the Age of Reform*, Burns and Innes, eds (Cambridge: Cambridge University Press, 2003), 254–70). This sense of crisis, one which Ruskin shares, led to a growing

interest in the neo-classical notion of art and art galleries as instruments of moral improvement (261).

31. Ruskin employs the term 'theoretic' to distinguish his position from early forms of aestheticism. See Nicholas Shrimpton's 'Ruskin and the Aesthetes', in *Ruskin and the Dawn of the Modern*, ed. Dinah Birch (Oxford: Oxford University Press, 1999), 134–5.

32. Ruskin, *Modern Painters, Vol. II*, 10.

33. This way of framing the nature of the beautiful and its relation to ethics (and theology) is obviously not a new one, and represents continuity with the Royal Academy tradition dominated by ideas put forth by Joshua Reynolds at the end of the eighteenth century. Wendell Harris describes the continuity between Ruskin and the Academic tradition: 'In terms of the moral value of art Ruskin did nothing to undercut the kind of latent Platonism that appears in Reynold's assumption that the beautiful is somehow both good in itself and productive of the good'. ('Ruskin's Theoretic Practicality and the Royal Academy's Aesthetic Idealism', *Nineteenth-Century Literature*, vol. 52, no. 1 (June 1997), 89)

34. Ruskin, *Modern Painters, Vol. II*, 17.

35. Ibid.

36. Ibid., 27.

37. Ibid.

38. Ibid., 29.

39. Ibid., 38.

40. Ibid., 29.

41. Ibid., 94.

42. Ibid., 38.

43. Ibid.

44. Ibid., 40.

45. As some of many examples, see the penultimate paragraph of the *Logic*, Chapter 3 of *On Liberty* and comments in 'Theism' (*Collected Works*, X:484–5).

46. Ruskin, *Modern Painters, Vol. II*, 73.

47. Ibid., 84.

48. Ibid., 87.

49. Ibid., 89.

50. Ibid., 90.

51. For an interesting treatment of the relationship between aesthetic appreciation of art and nature, see Allen Carlson, 'Appreciating art and appreciating nature', in *Landscape, natural beauty and the arts*, Salim Kemal and Ivan Gaskell, eds (Cambridge: Cambridge University Press, 1993), 199–227.

52. Ruskin, *Modern Painters, Vol. II*, 173. For a similar view in Mill, see 'Milne's poetry' (*Collected Works*, I:509).
53. This helps to explain Ruskin's frequent jibes against his Gradgrindian caricature of utilitarianism – a caricature that Mill detested, and yet found some truth in. That Ruskin was such a strong opponent of utilitarianism, as he understood it, and of associationism, makes Mill's praise of him all that much more remarkable.
54. Ruskin, *Modern Painters, Vol. II*, 24.
55. Ibid. The appropriateness of submitting ourselves to authority is demonstrated in our learning of any complex practice: chess playing, the violin, a martial art. The difficulty, as Ruskin points out, is knowing the balance between proper submission, stumbling about because one has ignored received wisdom, and being a slave to custom.
56. In 'Thoughts ...', Mill contends that the 'distinction between poetry and what is not poetry, whether explained or not, is felt to be fundamental: and where every one feels a difference, a difference there must be. All other appearances may be fallacious, but the appearance of a difference is a real difference' (*Collected Works*, I:343).
57. John Stuart Mill in James Mill, *An Analysis of the Phenomena of the Human Mind*, II:247.
58. Ibid., II:242.
59. Ibid. Interestingly, this seems to represent something of a change in his judgement of Mozart since his youthful writings. Whereas before Mozart was the great poet of musicians, now his music is presented as excelling, not in the expression of emotion, which is where the true poetry would lie, but in its merely sensual aspect.
60. Ibid., II:253.
61. Ibid., II:254.
62. Ibid., II:255.
63. Though Mill speaks of divine perfection with much more reticence than Ruskin, the operative general principles are the same.
64. Ibid.
65. These passages, which have been sadly ignored in the growing mound of articles on the higher/lower pleasure distinction, could eventually, I believe, help to clear up some of the discussions about it. Susan Feagin has made one of the only serious attempts to incorporate Mill's aesthetics and the passages in the *Analysis* into a reading of higher and lower pleasures (see 'Mill and Edwards on the Higher Pleasures', *Philosophy* 58 (1983): 244–52). It is a good start. One caution, however, is that she has too quickly generalized, in my opinion, from the structure of aesthetic higher pleasures to that of higher pleasures broadly considered. Other than the problem of a

lack of textual evidence either way, it seems to be a theory which does not make appropriate phenomenological distinctions among possible sources of the higher pleasures like pleasures of friendship, moral feelings and intellectual pleasures. I find it hard to make sense of those pleasures with the notion of perfections alone, and I see no reason why Mill should be saddled with such a view.

66. Though it is difficult to see nature as the expression of feeling, as that would compromise a number of traditional understandings of God, particularly in the Christian tradition, it should be remembered that this does not undermine a basic similarity in the aesthetic experiences of nature and art for Mill. Again, this may be connected to a willingness to see nature, like the work of art, as a product of design.

67. Nicholas Shrimpton, 'Ruskin and the Aesthetes', 149.

68. Alan Ryan, *The Philosophy of John Stuart Mill* (London: MacMillan, 1970), 255. Nicholas Capaldi, in his *John Stuart Mill: A Biography* (Cambridge: Cambridge University Press, 2004), ends his preface with the claim that Mill 'constructed a life that strove to be a Romantic work of art'.

69. Mill, *Collected Works*, XXI:256.

70. Mill, *Collected Works*, XVIII:263.

71. Mill, *Collected Works*, XXI:256.

72. Mill, *Collected Works*, XXI:255–6.

73. Mill, *Collected Works*, XXVII:643.

74. Mill, *Collected Works*, XXI:254.

75. Mill, *Collected Works*, XXI:255.

76. As Mill states in writings on the Gorgias, what makes Plato a 'great moral writer' and like a poet or an artist is his capacity to paint vivid portraits of moral heroes. The reader is brought into a love of 'noble feelings' by having his/her feelings and imagination guided by the 'moral artist'. See Mill, *Collected Works*, XI:150.

77. Mill, *Collected Works*, XXI:256.

78. On this point, see Alasdair MacIntyre, *After Virtue*, 2nd edn (Notre Dame, IN: University of Notre Dame Press, 1984), 198.

79. This also suggests that Ryan and numerous other critics may be mistaken in separating too sharply the pursuit of life as art and the project of social organization. In other words, on this view, the latter is seen as prior to life as art and as establishing constraints on how the individual pursues such a life. This is a reading which obviously places a great deal of weight on particular passages in *On Liberty*. Careful attention to texts such as *Principles of Political Economy* suggest an alternative picture, in which reformed institutions serve to foster and support individuals in treating their lives as works

of art. Not only do reformed institutions support such lives, but they are also necessary for them.

80. Wilhelm von Humboldt, *The Limits of State Action*, trans. J. W. Burrow (Indianapolis, IN: Liberty Fund, 1993), 18. For the rejection of utilitarianism by late-eighteenth century German liberal perfectionists like Humboldt, see Frederick Beiser, *Enlightenment, Revolution, & Romanticism* (Cambridge, MA: Harvard University Press, 1992), 20–1 and 131ff.

81. Mill often characterizes mass society in terms of 'slumber' and 'sleep'. The 'common herd' is in 'deep slumber' ('Aphorisms: Thoughts in the Cloister and the Crowd', in *Collected Works*, I:427). The poetic nature gets 'no rest' and life is easily made into a 'vale of tears' ('Writings of Alfred de Vigny', *Collected Works*, I:497). This holds, moreover, for the prophet Moses, whom Mill finds extremely well-captured in one of Vigny's poems: 'The theme is still the sufferings of the man of genius, the inspired man, the intellectual ruler and seer: not however, this time, the great man persecuted by the world, but the great man honoured by it, and in his natural place at the helm of it, he on whom all rely, whom all reverence – Moses on Pisgah, Moses the appointed of God, the judge, captain and hierarch of the chosen race—crying to God in anguish of spirit for deliverance and rest; that the cares and toils, the weariness and solitariness of heart, of him who is lifted altogether above his brethren, be no longer imposed on him—that the Almighty may withdraw his gifts, and suffer him to sleep the sleep of common humanity.' (I:500)

82. Mill, *Collected Works*, XXI:331.

83. Mill, *Collected Works*, XXI:332. Mrs. Grundy is, according to Susan Okin, 'a character in Thomas Morton's play *Speed the Plough* (1798), who represents the censoring opinions of the rigidly respectable'. See John Stuart Mill, *The Subjection of Women*, ed. Susan Okin (Indianapolis, IN: Hackett Publishing Company, 1988), 97.

84. Mill, *Collected Works*, XXI:332.

85. An interesting elucidation of these points can be found in 'Aphorisms: Thoughts in the Cloister and the Crowd', where Mill is commenting on a new work by Arthur Helps:

'The following is an observation of very great reach and importance:
It would often be as well to condemn a man unheard, as to condemn him upon the reasons which he openly avows for any course of action.
The explanation of this is to be found in another maxim of our author:
The reasons which any man offers to you for his own conduct betray his opinion of your character.
How true! how obvious! yet how seldom adverted to, and, we think, never written before. The reason which a man gives for his conduct is not

that which he feels, but that which he thinks you are most likely to feel. It often requires less moral courage to do a noble action than to avow that it proceeds from a noble motive. They who act on higher motives than the multitude suffer their conduct to be imputed to their personal position, to their friends, to their humour, even to some object of personal advancement—to anything, in short, which will not involve a reproach to others for not doing the like. They would rather the mean should think them as mean as themselves than incur the odium of setting up to be better than their neighbours, or the danger of giving others any cause to infer that they despise them.' (*Collected Works*, I:426)

86. Mill, *Collected Works*, XVIII:262.

87. Throughout his writings, but especially in Chapter 3 of *On Liberty*, Chapter 2 of *Utilitarianism* and his early essay 'On Genius' (*Collected Works*, I), Mill closely ties animal imagery to unthinking absorption in mass society. Sheep, cows, pigs, apes – along with steam engines, automatons and sundry other machines – are all paraded out as contrasts to the noble life of the authentic individual. Interestingly, the contrasts of animality with humanity and of mass consciousness with authentic individuality are replicated in the contrast of agreeableness with beauty. Only humans can experience the latter, and this experience depends not on associations that connect to everyday life, but on ones which direct us to a 'higher world'. Beauty is not only closely allied with individuality and humanity, it helps constitute them.

88. See 'Tennyson's Poems': 'Whoever, in the greatest concerns of human life, pursues truth with unbiassed feelings, and an intellect adequate to discern it, will not find that the resources of poetry are lost to him because he has learnt to use, and not abuse them. They are as open to him as they are to the sentimental weakling, who has no test of the true but the ornamental. And when he once has them under his command, he can wield them for purposes, and with a power, of which neither the dilettante nor the visionary have the slightest conception.' (*Collected Works*, I:417)

89. Mill, *Collected Works*, X:39.

2

Mill, Bentham, and 'Internal Culture'

In well-known lines from his *Autobiography*, Mill identifies two 'very marked effects' on his 'opinions and character' brought about by the period of his mental crisis.[1] The first involved no longer making happiness 'the direct end' of conduct and life. The second effect, which will consume our attention here, was that Mill 'gave its proper place, among the prime necessities of human well-being, to the internal culture of the individual', i.e. the cultivation of the feelings.[2] He had, he says, ceased to attach 'almost exclusive importance to the ordering of outward circumstances, and the training of the human being for speculation and for action'.[3]

The contrast of internal culture with speculation, action and 'the ordering of outward circumstances' draws on a vigorous literature of protest against the tenets of utilitarianism and political economy. Again and again in critics of utilitarianism like Carlyle, Coleridge, Dickens, Mackintosh, Matthew Arnold, and many evangelicals from the period, one finds defences of the 'inner', 'internal', 'interior', 'inward' and 'inmost' against the 'external', 'outward', 'outer' and the closely related 'mechanical'.[4] We can see a formidable and influential example of this genre in Carlyle's 'Signs of the Times', in which he identifies his era as a 'mechanical' one and makes the following lament:

> The Philosopher of this age is not a Socrates, a Plato, a Hooker, or Taylor, who inculcates on men the necessity and infinite worth of moral goodness, the great truth that our happiness depends on the mind which is within us, and not on the circumstances which are without us; but a Smith, a De Lolme, a Bentham, who chiefly inculcates the reverse of this,—that our happiness depends entirely on external circumstances; nay, that the strength and dignity of the mind within us is itself the creature and consequence of these. Were the laws, the government, in good order, all were well with us; the rest would care for itself![5]

This passage, though polemical and perhaps unfair, nevertheless hints at three basic and widespread complaints about the 'Philosophic Radicals' or Benthamites: 1) they simplify and flatten out our inner life by reducing human motivation to self-interest (often in service to developing a moral science of which the new political economy was a part), 2) they locate the sources of happiness primarily in 'external circumstances', like the services rendered by others, rather than in something less contingently related to the self, and 3) in morality, they prioritize action and 'underrate the importance of feeling and disposition'.[6] Thus, critics oppose the Philosophic Radicals in politics, which the radicals attempt to rationalize and turn into a science on the basis of controversial psychological premises, and in ethics, which, as Mackintosh put it, they treat 'too juridically'.[7]

These criticisms resonated strongly with Mill. Though he never fully abandons the tradition of his teachers, he worries about the lack of attention in Bentham's and his father's work to the quality of psychic life. The emphasis on internal culture in the passage from his *Autobiography* reflects Mill's reconsideration of 'philosophic radicalism' in the face of intelligent, aggressive, and hostile analysis.[8] This reconsideration focuses on character (or, more broadly, the self) and its education. Mill outlines a place for character in utilitarian theory and provides new goals for the development of various dispositions, especially those of feeling.

Studying these topics in Mill is of interest for a number of reasons. First, and most importantly, though what Mill has to say about character ideals is frequently mentioned in the secondary literature, *explanations* of what these ideals entail are much harder to come by. Taking 'internal culture' (or, for that matter, any of Mill's most popular phrases concerning character and human development) out of the realm of mere metaphor and into the realm of genuine philosophical concept is difficult. A phrase like 'internal culture' might sound suggestive, but what does it mean, and who would be against it? Until we can answer this kind of question, our understanding of Mill as ethicist – especially as advocate of norms for character education – will remain impoverished. One obstacle preventing an easy answer to this question is that internal culture, though an important idea in Mill's thought, remains more of a place-holder than a well-developed technical notion. He depends on his audience to understand what he means by it. For us to have access to it requires that we delve into the historical context within which he employs the idea. An examination of the debates in which Mill participated should allow us to make more sense of the philosophical point behind his appeal to internal culture.[9]

Second, this investigation provides us with an additional way of thinking about the meaning of Mill's famous confrontation with Coleridge and with associated currents in early- to mid-nineteenth-century thought. This confrontation made him reconceptualize utilitarian ethical theory and it drew his attention to anxieties concerning modern life that Bentham ignored.[10] Third, it offers a more articulate understanding of Mill as a reformer of political and social life, since much of his reforming work can be grasped only in relation to his commitments concerning character and its development. His justifications for the reform of institutions like the family and the workplace frequently centre on the impact of these institutions on the character of the people in them. Lastly, attention to the theme of internal culture makes Mill's ethical commitments more concrete, allowing us to evaluate him as a practicing ethicist, not merely as the defender of a version of the principle of utility.

I shall begin by presenting Bentham's views on internal culture, giving particular attention to the hopes (or lack thereof) Bentham had for affecting character, the ways in which he was most interested in doing so (largely tied to institutional reform), and the reasons that should prevent us from endorsing ambitious ideals of character development. The three criticisms of Bentham mentioned above turn out to be reasonably fair statements of the most important points of difference between Bentham and his opponents. I shall then look at the condemnation of 'mechanical' thought that spurred Mill's discussion of internal culture. This will lead to an examination of how Mill's conception of internal culture acts to address the three basic criticisms of Bentham's theory.

Bentham and internal culture

In his *Principles of Penal Law*, Bentham employs a metaphor which sheds light on his general orientation towards the feelings (in this case, the passions) and towards their organization in character. After suggesting that the 'seeds of good and evil are inseparably mixed' in the structure of human motivation, that there are no passions which are 'absolutely bad', and that context or situation will most often determine the actions to which the motives lead, he compares finding a 'useful balance' among the passions to the successful use of dykes to irrigate land. He concludes by contending that 'the art of constructing dykes consists in not directly opposing the violence of the current, which would carry away every obstacle placed directly in its front'.[11]

The 'dykes' that legislation establishes are not primarily intended to modify the nature of the 'current', i.e. the character of the passions themselves. As Bentham puts it earlier in the same section: 'The object of direct legislation is to combat pernicious desires, by prohibitions and punishments directed against the hurtful acts to which those desires may give birth. The object of indirect legislation is to countermine their influence, by augmenting the force of the less dangerous desires which may enter into competition with them.'[12] Thus, direct legislation (e.g. laws forbidding certain conduct) operates on the basis of negative sanctions against the acts to which 'pernicious desires' lead. These sanctions do not attempt to change the desires – they combat them. Indirect legislation tries to lessen the likelihood that these desires will get expressed in behaviour by promoting, through sanctions, the pursuit of other, less harmful desires (e.g. love of entertainment and the arts). The passions are, therefore, not candidates for fundamental alteration according to this theory of legislation.[13] Bentham spurns efforts to change the affective make-up of a people because 1) any motive may lead to good or bad actions depending on circumstance, so to identify specific passions as having consistent negative utility is very difficult, 2) the steps required to lessen significantly the prevalence of a motive usually create more harm than good, and 3) the expectation that one might be able to change humans in this way is naive – better to just accept their eternally mixed nature and get rid of any utopian impulses we might harbour.

The 'dykes', then, have their effects on action, not on the passions directly. They productively channel passions through the mechanisms of self-interest and sanction. This emphasis on 'institutional machinery' reflects a set of fundamental premises in thinking about political and social life. There is scarcely any discussion of inculcating virtue in the citizenry. There is little interest shown in interiority at all – external *expression* of interiority in action is what matters. The provision of healthy contexts for action, i.e. ones which direct predominately self-interested actors under the sway of the great multiplicity of human passions towards publicly useful ends, is the primary desideratum for the legislator. A smoothly functioning municipal law leads to prosperity and to ever-increasing civilization.[14]

This embrace of institutional organization and rationalization gets much of its energy from the early utilitarian acceptance of self-interest as sufficiently dominating human psychology so that all analysis of group interactions should be elucidated in terms of it. Explaining moral life scientifically required this approach, as Bentham had learned from Helvetius and other radical French philosophers.[15] The accusation that utilitarianism embodied cold, calculating economic thinking has its source, in good measure, from the promotion of this thesis.

But the commitment to self-interest and institutional machinery was not the only driving force behind the 'externalism' of the secular utilitarians. Another is the belief, attacked by Carlyle in the passage above, that our happiness depends much more on the actions of others and on our material conditions than it does on our character. James Mill puts forward an externalist view on the sources of happiness with which Bentham would have been in substantial agreement:

> One remarkable thing is first of all to be noticed: the three, above named [Wealth, Power, Dignity], grand causes of our pleasures agree in this, that they all are the means of procuring for us the Services of our fellow-creatures, and themselves contribute to our pleasures in hardly any other way. It is obvious from this remark, that the grand cause of all our pleasures are the services of our fellow-creatures; since Wealth, Power, and Dignity, which appear to most people to sum up the means of human happiness, are nothing more than means of procuring these services. This is a fact of the highest possible importance, both in Morals, and in Philosophy.[16]

Here, James Mill moves away from the tradition that happiness depends primarily on our internal organization or character.[17] For the elder Mill, except insofar as internal organization impacts the likelihood of our receiving services from others or of our being able to look after our own interests (i.e. the cases of prudence and temperance), it remains a less important source of happiness than does external circumstance. As Halevy puts the point, 'The only pleasures which the Utilitarian moralist wished in the last analysis to take into account, were the pleasures which had their source not in the exercise of our mental habits, but in external causes, such as gifts, wages or rewards, those pleasures, in a word, which are included under jurisprudence and political economy.'[18]

Such a position naturally leads the utilitarian theorist to attend to institutional settings in order to facilitate a mutuality of service-giving, thus bolstering overall happiness. The marketplace is a paradigm, since an efficient market does the best possible job of satisfying the relevant desires of the people participating in it. It has the additional advantage of leading to services while not depending upon any more lofty motives than self-interest. Exchange thereby becomes the fundamental social relationship.[19]

Bentham's lack of interest in internal culture, then, derives partly from his commitment to self-interest, to institutional 'dykes', and to some form of this 'externalist' view on the sources of happiness. In addition, it also stems from distaste for defending grand ideals of character development. Perhaps one of the most useful and rhetorically effective renderings of this scepticism concerning character ideals is found in Macaulay, the poet, historian, and part-time critic of utilitarians. In an essay on Bacon (1837), Macaulay contrasts the Baconian approach with that of the ancient moralists, in a way that captures the practical, anti-perfectionist and technical spirit which many of the Whig authors in the *Edinburgh Review*, for all their differences with the Philosophic Radicals, shared with Bentham and others like him:

> To sum up the whole, we should say that the aim of the Platonic philosophy was to exalt man into a god. The aim of the Baconian philosophy was to provide man with what he requires while he continues to be man. The aim of the Platonic philosophy was to raise us far above vulgar wants. The aim of the Baconian philosophy was to supply our vulgar wants. The former aim was noble; but the latter was attainable ... The philosophy of Plato began in words and ended in words, noble words indeed, words such as were to be expected from the finest of human intellects exercising boundless dominion over the finest of human languages. The philosophy of Bacon began in observations and ended in arts.
>
> The boast of the ancient philosophers was that their doctrine formed the minds of men to a high degree of wisdom and virtue. This was indeed the only practical good which the most celebrated of those teachers even pretended to effect; and undoubtedly, if they had effected this, they would have deserved far higher praise than if they had discovered the most salutary medicines or constructed the

most powerful machines. But the truth is that, in those very matters in which alone they professed to do any good to mankind, in those very matters for the sake of which they neglected all the vulgar interests of mankind, they did nothing, or worse than nothing. They promised what was impracticable; they despised what was practicable; they filled the world with long words and long beards; and they left it as wicked and as ignorant as they found it.

An acre in Middlesex is better than a principality in Utopia.[20]

We should note a few points in relation to this passage. First, Macaulay's emphasis, like that of the utilitarians, is eminently practical and allergic to metaphysical extravagance. Suffering and satisfaction are incontrovertible realities, ones that can be affected through policy and human intervention. Our happiness is largely dependent upon our interactions with nature (i.e. diseases, etc.), with others, and with the institutions that make up our social and political existence. It does not seem dependent on whether or not we achieve 'enlightenment', on whether or not we read philosophy, or on whether or not we are lovers of poetry and the arts. Bacon's greatness lay in his capacity to recognize those 'parts of human nature which lie low, but which are not liable to change'.[21] Such a view combats temptations towards perfectionism or utopianism. This attitude is connected to a sanguine stance towards bourgeois culture. Bentham in particular has no problem with people harmlessly spending their time on entertainments.

We can, of course, direct people's actions through the mechanism of institutions and incentives (thus the use of Bentham's dyke imagery and his advocacy for the Panopticon). We can aid their action by enabling them to better realize their interests through education, and by increasing our control over the physical world. But we should not expect or desire to produce a Stoic sage. Moreover, merely holding that kind of ideal is counterproductive. First, because, as Macaulay contends, the ideal is false: 'We know indeed that the philosophers were no better than other men. From the testimony of friends as well as foes, from the confessions of Epictetus and Seneca, as well as from the sneers of Lucian and the fierce invectives of Juvenal, it is plain that these teachers of virtue had all the vices of their neighbours, with the additional vice of hypocrisy.'[22] Second, the ideal's prejudices undervalue certain types of pleasures.[23] Third, it serves to distract us from those things that we can actually accomplish to make our lives here a little easier.

What this means is not that Bentham dismissed the value of character education. It means that we need to get specific about what kind of development is called for and can be justified. For Bentham, the primary desiderata of character development are prudence (the ability to discern well the consequences of action) and self-control or temperance (the capacity to choose a greater future pleasure over the lesser, but more immediate, one). Bentham's expectations for education are thus very modest, and he harbours a thorough-going scepticism about claims that people ought to be compared and evaluated on the basis of some vision of human perfection (like that of the Stoic sage, the Christian saint, or the Romantic poet).[24] Moreover, he was always aware of the possibility that 'moral reform' can be used as a vehicle for simply imposing one's own tastes on others.[25]

A second point to be gleaned from this passage is that the pragmatism and anti-perfectionism emphasized by Bentham and Macaulay dovetails with Bentham's jurisprudential orientation. With little hope of and interest in reforming the inner world of human beings, external behaviour absorbs Bentham's attention and leads him to take action as the proper object of morality (this is why Mackintosh accuses him of treating ethics 'too juridically').

Finally, the utilitarian and Whig pragmatism expressed in Macaulay's writing represents a possible reply to Carlyle's complaint that Bentham and others look to 'external circumstances' to explain the presence or absence of happiness rather than to 'the mind which is within us'. This, as we have seen, is basically true. But why do they emphasize external circumstances? First of all, the radicals wanted reform. Emphasizing the importance of happiness's external conditions fits neatly with this political agenda. Secondly, this emphasis implies sensitivity to human dependence on circumstance and environment – those who think that individuals *as* individuals primarily determine their own well-being locate responsibility incorrectly. The blame rests neither in our stars nor in ourselves, but in the institutions that serve to regulate our interactions. Addressing the flaws in these institutions focuses us on the concrete and available ways in which we can alleviate suffering and promote pleasure.

Critics

As we've seen, Carlyle argued that his age was a 'mechanical' one in which thinkers like Bentham treated humans as components to be fitted into a smoothly working machine. People are thereby seen only from the outside, from an external point of view. The criticisms of Bentham's and others' 'mechanical' thought play an important role in the period's discussion of internal culture.

In using this disparaging term, intellectuals like Carlyle were influenced by, among other things, German Romanticism, Idealism, *Naturphilosophie*, and more home-grown intellectual movements (e.g. some strands of Anglicanism and Protestantism more generally).[26] A number of oppositions were built into this accusation, all of which depended on characterizing the mechanical as an imposition on something more authentic. First, there were basic contrasts of the mechanical with the organic and living. In epistemology and philosophy of mind/ psychology these contrasts manifest in the distinction between the analytic understanding and synthetic reason, with only the latter supplying the genuine knowledge of the whole needed to fully comprehend the parts grasped by understanding. Coleridge, who brought this distinction into prominence in Britain, consistently speaks of the 'dead' or 'abstract' understanding in contrast to 'living' reason. The methodological criticisms of associationism and of the Lockean tradition in psychology relate to this, as does the rejection of self-interest as the key to interpreting action and institutions.

The necessity of knowing the whole if the part is to make sense also played out in historiography. Coleridge criticizes the 'histories and political economy of the present and preceding century' which 'partake in the general contagion of its mechanic philosophy, and are the product of an unenlivened generalizing understanding'.[27] Carlyle, mining a parallel vein, suggests that though history can never be fully interpreted by man, one may still distinguish 'the Artist in History ... from the Artisan in History; for here as in all other provinces, there are Artists and Artisans; men who labour mechanically in a department, without eye for the Whole, not feeling that there is a Whole; and men who inform and ennoble the humblest department with an Idea of the Whole, and habitually know that only in the Whole is the Partial to be truly discerned'.[28]

The charge of mechanism reflected not only specific epistemic, psycho-logical and, especially in the cases when it was motivated by religious criticism, metaphysical concerns, but it also gave voice to a general uneasiness about the impact of industrialism on feeling and about Enlightenment attitudes towards humanity (including the attempt to create a 'science of man'). Sussman finds hand-wringing about the relation of industrialism and humanity infusing the Victorian intellectual milieu: 'Combined with the use of the machine as metonymy for progress was another perception ... that the rhythms created by the machine itself had a profound and primarily destructive effect on the psychic life. This idea, that as mechanization expands the affective life declines, shapes the form as well as the content of much Victorian writing.'[29]

This basic stance, which tended to align the forces of interiority (i.e. art, imagination and religion) against industrial society and the philosophy of mechanism, can be found in numerous places, including Carlyle's essays, 'Signs of the Times' and 'Characteristics', where he discusses the 'mechanical' philosophy of utilitarianism, the caricatured Mr Gradgrind of Dickens' *Hard Times*, and Arnold's later *Culture and Anarchy*, where he speaks of 'the believer in machinery' as an enemy of culture and where he situates Bentham in the vanguard of the Philistines (in other words, the vanguard of the bourgeois middle classes).[30] Perhaps most tellingly, Mill recounts that his good friend John Sterling had, before knowing Mill well, accepted a common opinion that Mill was 'a "made" or manufactured man'.[31]

One of the more interesting examples of a critique of utilitarianism as a mechanical philosophy, however, and one which demonstrates the historical inertia of this association, comes from the 1880s and Lecky's *History of the Rise and Influence of the Spirit of Rationalism in Europe*. Lecky argues that utilitarianism is the 'philosophical expression of industri-alism'.[32] The perfection of individuals is subordinated in industrialism to the perfection of institutions ('externalism'): 'Among the moderns ... the law of development has been much more social than individual, and depends, as we have seen, on the growth of the industrial element.'[33] He contrasts the industrial spirit both with asceticism and with the Greek focus on individual perfection and the achievement of 'harmonious sustained manhood, without disproportion, or anomaly, or eccentricity'.

Lecky goes on to contend that utilitarianism has had immense impor-tance in 'correcting the evils of fanaticism, in calling into action the faculties which asceticism had petrified, and in furnishing a simple, universal principle of life'.[34] Thus, he is in basic agreement with Macaulay's praises of Baconian philosophy. But he argues that the defects of utilitarianism mirror the defects of rationalism and the associated modern, industrial spirit. Utility, though it is 'the highest motive to which reason can attain', cannot account for 'the noblest thing we possess, the celestial spark that is within us, the impress of the divine image, the principle of every heroism'.[35]

Internal Culture

Mill's advocacy for internal culture and for a re-evaluation of the goals of character education (especially the goals for the cultivation of dispositions of feeling) was conditioned by a sympathetic attention to these criticisms of utilitarianism. As we proceed to outline themes relevant to internal culture, we will come to comprehend how these themes need to be seen in relation to these criticisms.

The next three sections will treat the problem of internal culture directly. The first will examine Mill's analysis of Bentham's ethical theory. In particular, it will show that Mill took Bentham to task for having failed to properly incorporate the notion of character into his ethics. This created a lack of attention to interiority, including to the dispositions of feeling emphasized by the idea of internal culture. The second section will discuss Mill's treatment of aesthetic feeling – a category of feeling to which he assigns great value as a type of higher pleasure. I shall explain what makes aesthetic feeling or pleasure different from other kinds and show how, for Mill, the capacity to experience these pleasures is dependent upon the nature of one's character. The third section will study other feelings that Mill found wanting among his fellows, namely sympathetic feelings. In order to bring out more clearly some of the implications of Mill's views on internal culture, I shall go on to elucidate the means by which these feelings are cultivated in opposition to the tendencies of industrialism.

In each section, one finds Mill addressing the criticisms brought against Bentham's views. In the first, Mill implicitly responds to the claim that Bentham's treats ethics 'too juridically'. The second section characterizes anew the sources of happiness. Mill places more stress on sources of pleasure essentially dependent on the self (the 'inner'), rather than those sources which have only a contingent relation to the self and which depend more upon 'external circumstances'. The last section illustrates how Mill places greater emphasis on non-self-directed components of the human psyche (e.g. sympathy) than his early utilitarian companions.

Interiority and Ethics

In his different surveys of Bentham's ethical views, Mill is particularly keen to demand two revisions. First, he argues that Bentham fails to determine properly the consequences of actions due to his impoverished understanding of human psychology. For the calculation of consequences to be adequate one requires the science of ethology, i.e. the science of the formation of character.[36] The impact of actions on the human mind and on character must be understood in order to properly evaluate the actions' morality.[37]

A result of this lacuna in Bentham's theory – his 'ignorance of the deeper springs of human character' – is that it prevented him from appreciating the power of aesthetic activity to shape the moral nature of human beings.[38] To Bentham, the consequences of experiencing art are limited to the pleasures it produces. Thus, there is no reason to favour watching an Ibsen drama over playing solitaire if they produce equal pleasure. He gives short shrift to the possibility that art may have long-term impact on the sensibility of the spectator. This helps to explain Bentham's 'peculiar opinions on poetry', which contrast so sharply with Mill's emphasis on the arts as vital for the development of character, especially for the cultivation of feelings and imagination.

Mill's second revision of Bentham is related to the first and stems from his contention that the kinds of ethical evaluations demanded by Bentham's theory are insufficient. He criticizes Bentham in his essay 'Bentham' and in *Utilitarianism* for ignoring the 'sympathetic' and 'aesthetic' features of actions in favour of an exclusive focus on the 'moral' features of actions, and suggests that this gave 'to his philosophy that cold, mechanical and ungenial air which characterizes the popular idea of a Benthamite'.[39] The moral aspect, to which Bentham attends, provokes our reason and conscience to judge an action's rightness or wrongness (through its consequences), and results in moral approval and disapproval. The aesthetic aspect grounds judgements of beauty and ugliness, according to which we admire or despise. Our imagination plays the decisive role here. Lastly, judgements of love, pity or dislike, which are determined by 'human fellow-feeling', depend upon the sympathetic aspect of the act.[40]

Bentham, then, not only miscalculates the consequences of actions, but he also fails to notice that the specific consequences of an act are *not sufficient* to explain the evaluations that arise, and that ought to arise, in the face of it. What Bentham and other utilitarians ignore are those ethical judgements that have as their objects something other than the consequences of an act.[41] 'The morality of an action depends on its forseeable consequences; its beauty, and its loveableness, or the reverse, depend on the qualities which it is evidence of.'[42] Judgements of admiration or dislike or pity cover the dispositional *causes* of an action rather than the action's *results*. They are, in other words, 'backward-looking' rather than 'forward-looking' evaluations.

In the early essay 'Remarks on Bentham's Philosophy' (1833), which is a very good source for understanding Mill's ethical views, he expands on this point:

A certain kind of action, as for example, theft, or lying, would, if commonly practised, occasion certain evil consequences to society: but those evil consequences are far from constituting the entire moral bearings of the vices of theft or lying. We shall have a very imperfect view of the relation of those practices to the general happiness, if we suppose them to exist singly, and insulated. All acts suppose certain dispositions, and habits of mind and heart, which may be in themselves states of enjoyment or of wretchedness, and which must be fruitful in *other* consequences, besides those particular acts. No person can be a thief or a liar without being much else: and if our moral judgments and feelings with respect to a person convicted of either vice, were grounded solely upon the pernicious tendency of thieving and of lying, they would be partial and incomplete; many considerations would be omitted, which are at least equally "germane to the matter;" many which, by leaving them out of our general views, we may indeed teach ourselves a habit of overlooking, but which it is impossible for any of us not to be influenced by, in particular cases, in proportion as they are forced upon our attention.[43]

Beyond noticing from this passage that the Benthamites had developed a 'habit of overlooking' the aesthetic and sympathetic aspects of actions, we can uncover a Millian interest in establishing a sharp division between legislation and ethics. In legislation, the focus on the specific consequences of an action rather than on 'its general bearings upon the entire moral being of the agent' is appropriate.[44] 'The legislator enjoins or prohibits an action, with very little regard to the general moral excellence or turpitude which it implies; he looks to the consequences to society of the particular kind of action; his object is not to render people incapable of *desiring* a crime, but to deter them from actually *committing* it.'[45] Legislators, in other words, should concern themselves primarily with external behaviour; and in determining which acts to prohibit, they properly limit their attention to the consequences of the act alone.[46]

In ethics, on the other hand, this kind of attention is insufficient. Mill, three years after Mackintosh's critical *Encyclopedia Britannica* entry (see note 6), also interprets Bentham's ethical position as being too juridical. Ethical evaluation demands more than legislative evaluation does; it requires a careful consideration of character, of the *interiority* of which action is an *expression*. Exclusive attention to right and wrong means, for a utilitarian, exclusive attention to the consequences of a class of action. When we take into consideration the whole of ethical life, this attention leads us to ignore the importance of the claim that 'no person can be a thief or a liar without being much else'. Mill expresses this in the following account of Bentham's 'great fault ... as a moral philosopher':

> He has largely exemplified, and contributed very widely to diffuse, a tone of thinking, according to which any kind of action or any habit, which in its own specific consequences cannot be proved to be necessarily or probably productive of unhappiness to the agent himself or to others, is supposed to be fully justified; and any disapprobation or aversion entertained towards the individual by reason of it, is set down from that time forward as prejudice and superstition. It is not considered (at least, not habitually considered,) whether the act or habit in question, though not in itself necessarily pernicious, may not form part of a *character* essentially pernicious, or at least essentially deficient in some quality eminently conducive to the 'greatest happiness'.[47]

Mill wants the reader to recognize the undesirability of atomizing action and habit for the purposes of evaluation and to see how interconnected aspects of character can be. We cannot be habitual liars without being many other things besides (e.g. inconstant). The propensities to lie or to prefer push-pin to poetry, he suggests, cluster with other character traits, which may also properly influence our judgement of the action and of the dispositions which produce it. So though Bentham never ignores habits as potential sources of desirable and pernicious action (thus making them appropriate as objects of evaluation), he fails, according to Mill, to appreciate how habits relate to one's character as a whole.

We can now see how Mill's emphasis on internal culture represents, among other things, additional notice being given to the place of character in ethical theory (though Mill's position does not seem to attribute intrinsic value to states of character – he is still a utilitarian). Beyond the theoretical significance of this move, it is also an important precondition to greater interest in character education. One must assign weight to the place of character in ethics at large before turning character education into a significant ethical concern. Bringing character (the 'internal') into prominence is what Mill does in these analyses of Bentham's ethics.

Sources of happiness

Carlyle's proclamation of the 'great truth that our happiness depends on the mind which is within us, and not on the circumstances which are without us' resonates in Mill's treatment of aesthetic experience. Throughout his writings, Mill presents aesthetic experience as yielding a particularly valuable pleasure (i.e. a 'higher pleasure'), which is less dependent on 'external' sources than those pleasures emphasized by Bentham. The defence of 'internal' sources of happiness naturally leads to the problem of what internal states or dispositions produce this happiness. And, as we shall see, one's capacity to experience aesthetic pleasures has a non-contingent relation to one's character.

In his *Autobiography*, Mill broaches these themes in his account of how the arts yielded a solution to the problem at the heart of his youthful depression. In one well-noted discussion, he tells how he found a solution in Wordsworth's poetry, which presented 'not mere outward beauty, but states of feeling, and of thought coloured by feeling'. It was 'the very culture of the feelings, which I was in quest of. In them [Wordsworth's poems] I seemed to draw from *a source of inward joy*, of sympathetic and imaginative pleasure, which could be shared in by all human beings; which had no connexion with struggle or imperfection, but would be made richer by every improvement in the physical or social condition of mankind.'[48]

When searching through the text to find what 'state of ... thoughts and feelings' made the reading of Wordsworth helpful, we discover the following, which indicates that Mill judged 'external' sources of pleasure to be insufficient for happiness:

> I felt that the flaw in my life, must be a flaw in life itself: that the question was, whether, if the reformers of society and government could succeed in their objects, and every person in the community were free and in a state of physical comfort, the pleasures of life, being no longer kept up by struggle and privation, would cease to be pleasures. And I felt that unless I could see my way to some better hope than this for human happiness in general, my dejection must continue.[49]

Before the famous discussion of Wordsworth's healing effects, though, Mill remarks on the impact of another art: music. In a passage, to which less attention has been given, he claims that he felt relief that Weber's *Oberon* showed him to have a continuing susceptibility, even in his depression, to the pleasures of music. Mill goes on to suggest, however, that Weber did not help him as much as Wordsworth. The relief supplied by the music 'was much impaired by the thought, that the pleasure of music (as is quite true of such pleasure as this was, that of mere tune) fades with familiarity, and requires either to be revived by intermittance, or fed by continual novelty'.[50]

The key to comprehending Mill's appeals to art in the *Autobiography* and the implied contrast between the impact of Wordsworth and Weber is to attend carefully to the qualification given for the pleasure of Weber's music, namely that it is the pleasure of 'mere tune'. This is the fundamental problem. For the pleasure of mere tune, as we find out in the editorial notes for his father's *Analysis*, is a pleasure of sensation (i.e. pleasure caused by the sound itself), not a pleasure of expression (i.e. the associations connected to the sound).[51] Only the music which excels in expression can be considered truly poetic, that is, artistic. The other music, even if it is highly pleasurable, lacks depth. It is also, importantly, much more likely to be exhausted as a source of pleasure, needing to be 'revived by intermittance, or fed by continual novelty'.

Not all the things which produce pleasures of expression, however, are capable of being an 'inward source of joy'. Pleasures of expression that are merely pleasures of agreeableness, namely pleasures which result from association of an object to ideas of an everyday sort (e.g. children playing or a hot toddy in winter), remain insufficient. They are not aesthetic pleasures like those provided by Wordsworth's poetry. The feelings evoked by truly 'artistic' music and poetry have a phenomenological character – a certain kind of heft – that other feelings lack.[52]

Mill's explanation of this difference between the types of feeling rests, as we saw in Chapter 1, on a theory of the imagination (a theory partially influenced by Ruskin). In aesthetic experience, as opposed to the mere experience of the agreeable, we are carried by a work of art into a 'more majestic world'.[53] This means that we are confronted by or interact with various idealizations (of objects, virtues, etc.) or with the infinite. This confrontation with what Ruskin calls in the second volume of *Modern Painters* 'ideas of Beauty', accounts for the felt distinctness of experiences of the beautiful.[54]

If we ask why the pleasures of poetry or expressive music that go beyond mere agreeableness are different from the pleasures of 'mere tune', the answer is that art engages us with the ideal or infinite, that is, it brings us through webs of association into some kind of contact (e.g. conceptual, affective) with something apparently limitless or ideal. Music or poetry which depends on the 'physical' can do nothing of the kind.

This explains the inexhaustibility of the aesthetic pleasures. Whereas physical pleasures quickly reach a saturation point, at which time we often lose interest in them, imaginative pleasures of the sort we find in art can engage us in more sustainable ways. Contemplation of, or affective reaction to, the ideal or the infinite provides us with a permanent source of profound pleasure, which helped to assuage Mill's fears about the sources of pleasure available to humans. He had discovered a 'source of inward joy' distinct from those that produce pleasures of agreeableness or of sense.

Mill's crisis led him, or so he claims,[55] to the realization that our pleasures have different sources, and that they can have fundamentally different natures – a contention which the later higher/lower pleasure distinction in *Utilitarianism* can be fruitfully considered in relation to. This realization reconciled him to the view that the success of the reformer's project need not end in malaise, because the joy dependent on the internal state of the mind survives even when the pleasures dependent on political reform are gone.

The limiting condition to aesthetic pleasure is not simply exposure to or opportunity to confront the ideal or infinite. These are readily available. The capacity to enjoy these higher pleasures turns out to depend upon the presence of particular dispositions, upon the 'mind which is within us'. Thus we see how the debate surrounding the sources of human happiness connects directly to issues of character and internal culture.

Mill gives clues as to how aesthetic pleasure depends upon character in his essay 'Thoughts on Poetry and Its Varieties', discussed in Chapter 1, where he differentiates between the poetic and the narrative. There is a 'radical distinction between the interest felt in a story as such, and the interest excited by poetry; for the one is derived from incident, the other from the representation of feeling'.[56] Stories excite our emotions through showing 'states of mere outward circumstances', while the poetic excites through the 'exhibition of a state or states of human sensibility'.[57] Mill argues that these two sources of affective response – outward circumstance and human sensibility – 'correspond to *two distinct*, and (as respects their greatest development) *mutually exclusive, characters of mind*'.[58] Thus, a proneness to interest in stories reflects a lack of attention to interiority. Or, put another way, the person consistently attracted to story over poetry is one for whom 'inward joy' will be absent.

Mill presents the 'truth' of the story (and the knowledge needed by the novel-writer) as the truth available to the 'men of the world'.[59] Presumably these truths, having their source in 'outward experience', are forms of prudential knowledge concerning how to get things done, how to comport oneself in social life, with special focus on how we present ourselves to the world. This is, among other things, indicative of business savvy and practical success – success in *action*.

Stories, moreover, characteristically please children. The passion for stories is most intense in childhood, because the feelings depicted in stories and elicited by stories (at least of the sort Mill has in mind) are 'the simplest our nature has'.[60] The incidents of stories provoke 'such joys and griefs as the immediate pressure of some outward event excites in rude minds, which live wholly immersed in outward things, and have never, either from choice or a force they could not resist, turned themselves to the contemplation of the world within'.[61] Ordinary life interests us, provokes us, forces us to respond, but does nothing to connect itself to the ideal or the infinite. It is obvious. It is transparent. Events are interpreted using the ready-made categories of a language community, and these categories condition the response of children to the stories. In fact, storytelling involves one of the first introductions of these social norms and categories to children.

What we find, then, are that the two sources of interest – poetry and narrative – depend for the pleasures they produce on two contrasting dispositions of imagination and feeling. Narrative draws on those imaginations and feelings grabbed by action and by 'outward things'. The narrative mind is the mind of industrial society. It is quickly aroused and absorbed in the excitement of stories, but these stories leave little behind them to engage it. The 'joys and griefs' which 'outward events' excite satisfy the narrative mind, and it lacks the capacity of the imagination needed to rise to a 'more majestic world', which might provide it with other, higher pleasures. The poetic mind, on the other hand, due to its powers of imagination, finds pleasure in the discovery of the ideal and the infinite. It rejects the speed and exhilaration of industry in order to tarry with the aesthetic (and frequently pastoral) object. The 'internal' character of the feelings associated with poetry such as Wordsworth's derives from its relation to self-reflection and from its connection, through imagination, to ideal and infinite aspects of the world and the self hidden by the 'external' goings-on of social existence in industrial society.

The pleasures of sympathy

The last revision of Bentham triggered by criticism and embodied in Mill's highlighting of internal culture involves the rejection of a central feature of Bentham's moral psychology – its reduction of almost all motivation to some form of self-interest. This moral psychology reflected an ambition found in the radical French Enlightenment and in the developing field of Political Economy (Bentham was a great admirer of Smith's *Wealth of Nations* and also closely linked to Ricardo through the mediation of James Mill), namely the ambition to explain human behaviour as a class of natural phenomena subject to laws. In other words, he was attracted to the idea of establishing a 'science of man', and the premise that human action is driven by self-interest seemed justified and useful in creating such a science.[62]

To Bentham's opponents, the emphasis on self-interest showed how impoverished the utilitarian understanding of the 'internal' was. The utilitarian inner life is not a site of deep conflict or wonder, nor is it, because of that, a site of genuine ethical interest for another; it is comprehensible and consistently directed. The form that a utilitarian life takes depends more on dealing with external obstacles to satisfaction and less on struggling with the complexities of one's psyche, including, in the view of the critics, the multiplicity of human motivations.

For Mill, Bentham's account of human motivation was not only incorrect, but it also had pernicious effects in the realm of moral education, because it 1) blinded the utilitarians to the importance of sympathy both for social life and for the well-being of the individual, and 2) exacerbated a sharpening decline in sympathetic relations with others by ignoring those features of others (e.g. the complexity of motivations) that might engage us and make us more prone to sympathize. The marginalization of sympathy and the pleasures associated with it was a problem that went beyond the secular utilitarians, however. Mill thought it endemic to English life as a whole. This problem – the absence of warmth and sympathetic feelings – served to fuel the literature on the evils of the mechanical and industrial spirit and on the way in which modern societal relations were founded on cash and contract, rather than on intimacy and emotional connection. Driven by these criticisms, Mill diagnosed the causes of this lack of pleasure in sympathy and suggested some ways to remedy it.

In discussing the negative attitude of one of his earlier intellectual companions, J. A. Roebuck, towards the cultivation of sympathies and feelings through art, Mill says that Roebuck 'like most Englishmen who have feelings … found his feelings stand very much in his way. He was much more susceptible to the painful sympathies than to the pleasurable, and looking for his happiness elsewhere, he wished that his feelings should be deadened rather than quickened.'[63] Roebuck's stance reflected the deeper structure of English life, because 'in truth, the English character, and the English social circumstances, make it so seldom possible to derive happiness from the exercise of the sympathies, that it is not wonderful if they count for little in an Englishman's scheme of life'.[64] As opposed to those in other countries, particularly in France, for whom the sympathies are of paramount importance for individual happiness, many Englishmen 'almost seem to regard them as necessary evils, required for keeping men's actions benevolent and compassionate'.[65] That is, the English (and here Mill sees Bentham as the paradigmatic Englishman), might think the sympathies are important insofar as they support the performance of duty. But beyond that, they are often more trouble than they are worth.

The English inability to experience pleasure through sympathetic connection with others depends on three different sources. The first, which comes to light particularly in Mill's discussion of his father's aversion to the expression of feeling, is what might loosely be called English stoicism. James Mill 'resembled most Englishmen in being ashamed of the signs of feeling, and by the absence of demonstration, starving the feelings themselves'.[66] The dominant ethos is a form of self-command. As such, expressions of feeling can be seen as extravagant, and, to bring gender into it, as womanly. To sympathize or feel with others and to express it would be more an occasion of pain than of pleasure, because the feelings are taken by both parties to be embarrassments. They are signs of a lack of seriousness and of an unseemly susceptibility to changes in environment.

In the 'Inaugural Address Delivered to the University of St. Andrews', Mill identifies the other two sources. While speaking of why the British take art less seriously than those on the Continent (particularly those in France and Germany), he argues that the British failure to count the arts among the 'great social powers' and the 'agents of civilization' 'may be traced to the two influences which have chiefly shaped the British character since the days of the Stuarts; commercial money-getting business, and religious Puritanism'.[67]

Puritanism 'looked coldly, if not disapprovingly, on the cultivation of the sentiments'. This Puritanism, which Mill in other places identifies as a form of Calvinism, interprets emotion as generally tied to corporeality and to sin. Matthew Arnold was among those Victorians who joined Mill in accusing Puritanism of stunting human development.[68]

The most important cause, for our purposes, of the English inability to experience pleasure in the sympathies is commercial society. Here, there is not a general attack on the affections, as there is in English stoicism and Puritanism. Rather, money-getting tends to incorporate all other pursuits, making them instrumental to the end of increasing wealth. This commercialism has the dual effect of promoting the English sensitivity to violations of duty (i.e. conscience: 'the kind of advantage which we have had over many other countries in point of morals'),[69] while leaving nothing to oppose self-interested behaviour. We find in the 'Inaugural Address' the negative impact this can have on character:

> One of the commonest types of character among us is that of a man all whose ambition is self-regarding; who has no higher purpose in life than to enrich or raise in the world himself and his family; who never dreams of making the good of his fellow-creatures or of his country an habitual object, further than giving away, annually or from time to time, certain sums in charity; but who has a conscience sincerely alive to whatever is generally considered wrong, and would scruple to use any very illegitimate means for attaining his self-interested objects.[70]

This character type emphasizes the Englishman as commercial man, as pursuing self-interested objects (including those of family) but in ways that do not disturb social stability. He is a respecter of rules, and since robust feelings often lead to the transgression of those rules and the disruption of expectation, feelings are devalued.

How, then, does one address that impoverishment of the 'internal' indicated by a lack of sympathetic feelings and pleasures? How does one generate enough interest in or concern for the other to promote pleasure in sympathy? In other words, what would this part of internal culture look like? Mill turns primarily to the cultivated imagination as embodied in art and history. We can begin understanding what this might mean by looking at what Mill has to say about how the 'exclusive cultivation' of 'habits of analysis and abstraction',

> while it strengthens the associations which connect means with ends, effects with causes, tends to weaken many of those upon which our enjoyments and our social feelings depend; and by accustoming the mind to consider, in objects, chiefly the properties on account of which we refer them to classes and give them general names, leaves our conceptions of them as individuals, lame and meager:—how, therefore, the corrective and antagonist principle to the pursuits which deal with objects only in the abstract, is to be sought in those which deal with them altogether in the concrete, clothed in properties and circumstances: real life in its most varied forms, poetry and art in all their branches.[71]

This passage shows that one of the most important ways in which the social feelings are supported (and in which the 'dissolving force of analysis'[72] that prompted Mill's crisis is combated) is through being able to see objects and people 'in the concrete' rather than as types or as one in a series of causes and effects (a point of view promoted by industrialism). Doing this depends on the imagination.

The pleasures of sympathy require an activity of the imagination which is different from that responsible for aesthetic pleasures, but one which Mill still consistently describes as 'aesthetic' or 'poetic'. It might best be called 'concretization' or the taking up of various aspects of a thing not present and tying them together into an image of a convincing, real unity, which can more thoroughly act upon our feelings and motivations. This is one of the main functions of the imagination, 'which Bentham had not'.[73] The imagination 'enables us, by a voluntary effort, to conceive the absent as if it were present, the imaginary as if it were real, and to clothe it in the feelings which, if it were indeed real, it would bring along with it. This is the power by which one human being enters into the mind and circumstances of another.'[74] It is what constitutes the poet, dramatist and historian: through successful employment of the force of their imaginations, they are able to make something or someone real or particular enough to engage the sympathies.

We can better understand how one cultivates the 'concretizing' imagination necessary for promoting sympathy in an industrializing world by looking at Mill's discussion of history, drama and poetry. His review 'Carlyle's French Revolution' (1837) begins by proclaiming about Carlyle's work that 'This is not so much a history, as an epic poem; and notwithstanding, or even in consequence of this, the truest of histories. It is the history of the French Revolution, and the poetry of it, both in one.'[75] Mill contrasts the poetry of Carlyle's history with the psychological flatness of some of Britain's greatest eighteenth-century historians (and one must wonder whether his father's *History of British India* might also fall under the scope of this criticism):

> If there be a person who, in reading the histories of Hume, Robertson, and Gibbon (works of extraordinary talent, and the works of great writers) has never felt that this, after all, is not history—and that the lives and deeds of his fellow-creatures must be placed before him in quite another manner, if he is to know them, or feel them to be real beings, who once were alive, beings of his own flesh and blood, not mere shadows and dim abstractions; such a person, for whom plausible

talk *about* a thing does as well as an image of the thing itself, feels no
need of a book like Mr. Carlyle's.[76]

Mill goes on to note how the want for something beyond 'shadows and dim
abstractions' is 'generally felt', and how this can be seen from the popularity
of historical plays and romances. One can be responsive to 'authentic facts'
while still creating a history with blood coursing through it.

Mill further sharpens his distinction between poetic and non-poetic
histories by comparing Carlyle's history with the work of dramatists such
as Schiller and Vitet. But he leaves his most illuminating comparison for
Shakespeare:

> It has been noted as a point which distinguishes Shakespeare from
> ordinary dramatists, that *their* characters are logical abstractions, his
> are human beings: that their kings are nothing but kings, their lovers
> nothing but lovers, their patriots, courtiers, villains, cowards, bullies,
> are each of them that, and that alone; while his are real men and
> women, who have these qualities, but have them in addition to their
> full share of all other qualities (not incompatible), which are incident to
> human nature. In Shakespeare, consequently, we feel we are in a world
> of realities; *we are among such beings as really could exist, as do exist, or have
> existed, and as we can sympathise with*; the faces around us are human faces,
> and not mere rudiments of such, or exaggerations of single features.
> This quality, so often pointed out as distinctive of Shakespeare's plays,
> distinguishes Mr. Carlyle's history.[77]

The ordinary dramatist (and historian) fails to make his characters more
than marginally sympathetic, because the characters are nothing more
than one role (e.g. king, villain, courtier), rather than a person with
complex motivations and complex conflicts among roles. If the character
acts in a way not included within our understanding of that one role, the
action loses an intelligible relation to the actor. Shakespeare's Prince Hal,
by contrast, is not merely the embodiment of the audience's stereotype of
a prince; he is a son, a friend, a ne'r-do-well. As such, his humanity and
his interiority, including the exercise of his judgement and the process of
his making choices, become more and more apparent to us. The flatness
of a mere prince is replaced by the fullness of a person.

For the historian, then, enabling the reader to 'picture to himself what
human life was' in any particular historical period is the most basic

requirement for engaging the reader's sympathies. By giving a sense for the joys, sorrows, hopes, fears, ideas and opinions of a people (including not merely the nobility, but the commoners), one comes to understand the reasons why individuals or groups acted as they did. In so doing, we are better situated to sympathize potentially with the actors and 'to erect ourselves into judges' of conduct.[78] A more 'objective', fact-based historical approach, including political and military histories, becomes, under this view, less fundamental than various forms of cultural history.

Thus we see that sympathetic pleasures, and the feeling of unity with others which depends upon these pleasures, itself depends on a particular kind of imaginative capability – a capability that turns people from mere types into concrete individuals with whom we may more readily share affective bonds. This is an imaginative disposition that history and art, which are among the 'great social powers' and 'agents of civilization', serve to cultivate. It is also a disposition that industrialism, according to Mill and other thinkers of the period, deadens. People become means for realizing ends, or cogs in institutional machines, rather than beings in themselves worthy of attention. The conflict of the internal versus the external has one of its decisive engagements in the realm of the sympathies. Whether the internal succumbs or emerges victorious depends in part on how the skirmish between the poetic and the industrial turns out. Mill took the deadening of sympathies in England to be a sign of the undesirable dominance of the latter over the former.

Conclusion

It has often been noticed, especially in discussions concerning *On Liberty*, that Mill places great emphasis on moral education and self-cultivation. It has been rarely made clear in specific terms, however, what Mill's commitment to education amounts to. How should we understand his position?

The heightened attention to the dichotomy of internal/external in early- to mid-nineteenth-century Britain reflected numerous concerns. As I have shown, critics of utilitarians emphasized the importance of representing inner life with a complex palette of motives and of recognizing how human happiness often depends more on factors essential to the self (e.g. dispositions of imagination and feeling) than on those that are contingently related to it (e.g. the quality of the legal system). They also argued for the centrality of character and feelings (e.g. aesthetic and sympathetic) to ethical theory.

Mill's reform of utilitarian ethics indicates his awareness of Bentham's shortcomings as an ethicist and of the legitimacy of the critics' anxieties about the impact of accelerating social, political and economic changes on the psyche. He is engaged in articulating a vision for how human development should advance, along with making scientific claims about the conditions for the possibility of this development – claims detailed in his more sociological works like *Subjection of Women* and *Principles of Political Economy*.

Mill's views on internal culture reveal some of the most important ways in which he conceptualized human interiority, both as it is and as he thought it should be. Studying these views furthers our appreciation of the specific connections between this conceptualization and the intellectual pressures exerted by critics of the period.

Endnotes

1. John Stuart Mill, *The Collected Works of John Stuart Mill*, gen. ed. John M. Robson, 33 vols (Toronto: University of Toronto Press, 1963–91), I:145.
2. Mill, *Collected Works*, I:147.
3. Ibid.
4. See Brian Harrison, 'State Intervention and Moral Reform in Nineteeth-century England' in Patricia Hollis (ed.), *Pressure from Without in Early Victorian England* (New York: St. Martin's Press, 1974), 289–322, in which he notes the concern for the 'regeneration of the inward man' and the use of 'outer' and 'inner' among dissenters, 296.
5. Thomas Carlyle, 'Signs of the Times' [1829] in *A Carlyle Reader*, ed. G. B. Tennyson (Cambridge: Cambridge University Press, 1984), 40–1. Matthew Arnold, 40 years later, echoes this same point, when he claims that culture is the study of a perfection which consists 'in becoming something rather than in having something, in an inward condition of the mind and spirit, not in an outward set of circumstances' (*Culture and Anarchy* (Cambridge: Cambridge University Press, 1969), 48). And Mill himself ends *On Liberty* by contrasting the development of individuality in a society with the interests of those who govern and want to have the 'machine ... work more smoothly'.
6. James Mackintosh, *Dissertation Second; Exhibiting a General View of the Progress*

of Ethical Philosophy, Chiefly During the Seventeenth and Eighteenth Centuries, prefixed to the seventh edition of the *Encyclopedia Britannica* [1830], 384.

7. Ibid.

8. Mill was not alone among the friends of utilitarianism on this score. In his *Autobiography* (I:185), he talks about his affinities with the elder Austin who had spent time in Germany: 'He attached much less importance than formerly to outward changes; unless accompanied by a better cultivation of the inward nature. He had a strong distaste for the general meanness of English life, the absence of enlarged thoughts and unselfish desires, the low objects on which the faculties of all classes of the English are intent.' These themes will emerge again in Chapter 3.

9. The few previous attempts to deal with the topic of internal culture in the philosophical literature tend to be cursory or to suffer from too much dependence on what Mill has to say without situating it sufficiently in its historical context. Prominent examples of the latter include the otherwise helpful book by Wendy Donner (*The Liberal Self* (Ithaca, NY: Cornell University Press, 1991), see especially Chapter 5), John Robson's 'J. S. Mill's Theory of Poetry' in *Mill: A Collection of Critical Essays*, ed. J. B. Schneewind (London: MacMillan, 1968), and his *The Improvement of Mankind* (London: University of Toronto Press, 1968), 25–30. Other treatments, though suggestive, are brief. See Alan Ryan, *J. S. Mill* (London: Routledge and Kegan Paul, 1974), 33 and 55, and Maurice Mandelbaum's excellent *History, Man, & Reason* (Baltimore, MD: Johns Hopkins Press, 1971), 194–7 and 213–14.

10. Skorupski nicely states the centrality of this confrontation of Enlightenment (Bentham) and Romanticism (Coleridge) for understanding Mill's thought:

> Mill's project, in most general terms, was to present the enlightenment perspective in a way which would claim the allegiance and enthusiasm of thinking men and women, and, through them, exercise a social authority for good. He wanted to rethink it in detail and to show how it could incorporate and transcend the criticisms which had been made of it in the age of early nineteenth-century romanticism, the age in which he grew to maturity. Accordingly, the deepest criticisms of Mill are those which argue that he failed in just this respect; that the enlightenment perspective as such is incoherent – in its metaphysics, or its politics, or both. A full appreciation of Mill requires that one recognise what issues are at stake here and why they are significant.

> John Skorupski, *John Stuart Mill* (London: Routledge, 1989), 2.

11. Jeremy Bentham, *The Works of Jeremy Bentham*, ed. John Bowring, 10 vols (New York: Russell and Russell, 1962), I:539. Beccaria, whose writings

exerted a very strong influence on Bentham, uses strikingly similar language:

> The force, like the force of gravity, which compels us to our own well-being, can be checked only by measure of the obstacles opposed to it. Its effects are the confused series of human actions. If these clash and impede one another, then punishments, which I would call political obstacles, prevent their bad effects without doing away with their compelling cause, which is the sensibility inseparable from man; and the lawmaker acts the part of the skillful architect, whose business it is to counteract the ruinating course of gravity and cause the interaction of all that contributes to the strength of his building.
>
> Cesare Beccaria, *Of Crimes and Punishments*, translated by Jane Grigson
> (New York: Marsilio Publishers, 1996), 75.

12. Ibid.

13. Bentham does make an exception here, however. He identifies three passions which a legislator should have interest in expunging: 1) the malevolent passions (e.g. ill-will, antipathy, malevolent or dissocial affections), 2) the fondness for inebriating liquors, and 3) the love of idleness, namely indolence. Of these three, the second has the unique distinction of being the only passion which may be extirpated 'without producing any evil', that is, it is the only passion Bentham recognizes which has no positive utility. As for the other two, indolence 'favours the ascendancy of evil passions', while the vindictive passions are disruptive of civilized social life. See Bentham, *Works*, I:539.

14. For a very helpful discussion of 'mechanical' political and social theories in British thought of the eighteenth and nineteenth centuries, see Stefan Collini, Donald Winch, and John Burrow, *That Noble Science of Politics* (Cambridge: Cambridge University Press, 1983). In a treatment of Hume's and Smith's assumption (employed by James Mill in his dispute with Macaulay and Mackintosh) that in politics one ought to consider every man a knave who has no other end in mind but his own self-interest, the authors suggest: 'The assumption that, by and large, self-interest rules collective behaviour in political as well as economic settings entailed giving greater emphasis to impersonal institutional machinery as a means of checking, balancing, and harnessing self-interest and containing its more destructive results' (30–1).

15. See, for example, Claude-Adrien Helvetius, *De L'Esprit* (Tours: Librairie Artheme Fayard, 1988), 59: 'Si l'Univers physique est soumis aux lois du movement, l'Univers moral ne l'est pas moins a celles de l'interet.'

16. James Mill, *An Analysis of the Phenomena of the Human Mind*, ed. John Stuart Mill, 2 vols (London: Longmans, Green and Dyer, 1869), II:208.

17. Perhaps because of his Scottish training for the ministry, James Mill seems to waver on these points occasionally in a way that Bentham never does.

18. Elie Halevy, *The Growth of Philosophical Radicalism*, trans. Mary Morris (Boston, MA: Beacon Press, 1955), 469.

19. Ibid., 470.

20. Thomas Macaulay, *Critical and Historical Essays*, 2 vols (London: Everyman's Library, 1937), II:373. Earlier, Bentham makes a similar point more directly: 'While Xenophon was writing History, and Euclid teaching Geometry, Socrates and Plato were talking nonsense, on pretence of teaching morality and wisdom. This morality of theirs consisted in words.' Jeremy Bentham, *Deontology together with A Table of the Springs of Action and The Article on Utilitarianism*, ed. Amnon Goldworth (Oxford: Clarendon Press, 1983), 135.

    For an additional example of Bentham's basic agreement with this view, see his claim in 'Of the Influence of Time and Place in Matters of Legislation': 'Let us seek only for what is attainable: it presents a career sufficiently vast for genius; sufficiently difficult for the exercise of the greatest virtues. We shall never make this world the abode of perfect happiness: when we shall have accomplished all that can be done, this paradise will be, according to the Asiatic idea, only a garden; but this garden will be a most delightful abode, compared with the savage forest in which men have so long wandered.' (Bentham, *Works*, I:194)

21. Macaulay, *Critical and Historical Essays*, II:376.

22. Ibid., 374. See also the following note from Bentham, included in 'Bentham's Conversation': 'Fanny Wright told me Socrates was pure as an icicle. I answered that it was my misfortune to read Greek, and to know better. What I read of Socrates was insipid. I could find in him nothing that distinguished him from other people except his manner of putting questions.' (Bentham, *Works*, X:583) One of the most interesting contrasts between Bentham and both Mills comes from their differing evaluation of Socrates.

23. On this point, see Bentham's critique of taste in the 'Rationale of Reward', *Works*, II:254, where he claims that it is 'only from custom and prejudice that, in matters of taste, we speak of false and true', and where he goes on to attack the presumption of critics who attempt to establish a hierarchy of pleasures.

24. The proper role of the moralist, as one can see in Bentham's *Deontology*, is the correction of mistakes concerning what constitutes one's real interest. For a good treatment of Bentham's moral theory, such as it is, see Ross Harrison, *Bentham* (London: Routledge and Kegan Paul, 1983), Chapter X.

25. There was a great interest in Moral Reform from 1780 to the early decades of the nineteenth century – perhaps this growing interest in moral reform contributed to Bentham's antipathy for it. See Joanna Innes, '"Reform" in English public life: the fortunes of a word' in *Rethinking the Age of Reform*, Arthur Burns and Joanna Innes, eds (Cambridge: Cambridge University Press, 2003), 93–4.

26. The opposition between inner and outer can be found in the German contrast of 'Kultur' (and the associated 'Bildung'), which expresses the value placed on the inner, spiritual sphere and its development, with 'Zivilisation', which is something of secondary importance, namely the outward appearance and form of human beings. For the seminal treatment of this distinction, see Norbert Elias, *The Civilizing Process* (Oxford: Blackwell Publishers, 1994), 3–9. Mandelbaum notes the importance of the 'inner' in German idealism: 'it constituted a reaction against the philosophy of positivism, asserting the claim that ultimate reality was accessible to man; however, it was claimed to be accessible only if man abandoned the equation of scientific knowledge with truth, looking inward rather than outward for the clues to that which lay behind the realm of nature with which science was destined to deal' (Mandelbaum, *History, Man, & Reason*, 10). This is a position, of course, that Mill vehemently rejects.

27. S. T. C. Coleridge, 'Lay Sermons' in *On the Constitution of the Church and State According to the Idea of Each (3rd Edition), and Lay Sermons (2nd Edition)* (London: William Pickering, 1839), 228.

28. Thomas Carlyle, 'On History' in *Critical and Miscellaneous Essays* (Philadelphia, PA: Casey and Hart, 1845), 222.

29. Herbert Sussman, *Victorians and the Machine* (Cambridge, MA: Harvard University Press, 1968), 4.

30. Matthew Arnold, *Culture and Anarchy and Other Writings* (Cambridge: Cambridge University Press, 1993), 13.

31. Mill, *Collected Works*, I:161.

32. William Lecky, *History of the Rise and Influence of the Spirit of Rationalism in Europe* (New York: D. Appleton and Company, 1888), 10.

33. Ibid., 351.

34. Ibid., 352.

35. Ibid., 353.

36. See Mill's *A System of Logic* (New York: Harper & Brothers, 1874), VI.5. Ethology is part of a far more complex conception of the moral sciences: 'And since it is by these laws [the universal laws of the formation of character] combined with the facts of each particular case, that the whole of the phenomena of human action and feeling are produced, it is on these

that every rational attempt to construct the science of human nature in the concrete, and for practical purposes, must proceed', (VI.5.2).

37. Mill attests to this in the following: 'Morality consists of two parts. One of these is self-education; the training, by the human being himself, of his affections and will. That department is a blank in Bentham's system. The other and co-equal part, the regulation of outward actions, must be altogether halting and imperfect without the first; for how can we judge in what manner many an action will affect even the worldly interests of ourselves or others, unless we take in, as part of the question, its influence on the regulation of our, or their, affections and desires?' Mill, *Collected Works*, X:98.

38. Mill, *Collected Works*, X:113.

39. Mill, *Collected Works*, X:112.

40. Ibid. See also Mill, *Collected Works*, X:221.

41. For the legitimacy of this as an interpretation of Bentham's ethical views, see Harrison's analysis of Bentham's 'deontology': Ross Harrison, *Bentham* (London: Routledge and Kegan Paul, 1983), 274.

42. Mill, *Collected Works*, X:112.

43. Mill, *Collected Works*, X:7.

44. Mill, *Collected Works*, X:8.

45. Mill, *Collected Works*, X:9.

46. We will see in Chapter 3, however, that Mill, later in his career, seems eager to expand the appropriate scope of legislation.

47. Mill, *Collected Works*, X:8.

48. Mill, *Collected Works*, I:151, italics added. This description of aesthetic pleasure also has obvious implications for thinking about class. Aesthetic pleasure is to be that which connects us, that which helps us overcome class conflict, etc. For an interesting Marxist interpretation of the political employment of the notion of the aesthetic, see Terry Eagleton, *The Ideology of the Aesthetic* (Oxford: Basil Blackwell, 1990).

49. Mill, *Collected Works*, I:149.

50. Ibid.

51. John Stuart Mill in James Mill, *An Analysis of the Phenomena of the Human Mind*, 2 vols, ed. John Stuart Mill (London: Longmans, Green and Dyer, 1869), II:241–2.

52. The distinction between the agreeable and the beautiful was a commonplace in the period. Mill accepts Coleridge's formulation of the issue, though he rejects his explanation of the differences between the feelings in favour of an associationist account. See John Stuart Mill in James Mill, *Analysis*, II: 252.

53. John Stuart Mill in James Mill, *Analysis*, II:255.

54. John Ruskin, *Modern Painters, Vol. 2* (New York: D. D. Merrill Company, 1893). Ruskin's project in this part of his multi-volume work is to catalogue the ideas of beauty (i.e. those ideas which are expressed by the aesthetic object and which are responsible for our experience of the beautiful), and to elucidate the workings and proper objects of the two central faculties for the creation and appreciation of art, namely the imagination and what he calls the 'theoretic faculty'.

55. Whether Mill's account of his crisis is true to life is not important for our purposes. What is important is how he explains the events to himself and to his readers. For one well-known revision of the history of Mill's crisis, see Michael Packe, *The Life of John Stuart Mill* (New York: MacMillan Company, 1954), 79–82.

56. Mill, *Collected Works*, I:344.

57. Mill, *Collected Works*, I:344–5. One can see here yet another incarnation of the language of inner/outer in the distinction between the poetic and the narrative. For an interesting use of these texts in a treatment of Mill's associationism, see Candace Vogler, *John Stuart Mill's Deliberative Landscape* (New York: Garland Publishing, 2001), Chapter 4.

58. Mill, *Collected Works*, I:345, italics added.

59. Mill, *Collected Works*, I:346.

60. Mill, *Collected Works*, I:345.

61. Ibid.

62. See note 15. Though Bentham mentions sympathy as a possible motivation for action, he rarely emphasizes it or makes the notion do much work.

63. Mill, *Collected Works*, I:157.

64. Ibid.

65. Ibid.

66. Mill, *Collected Works*, I:153.

67. Mill, *Collected Works*, XXI:253.

68. Arnold makes the point in his own idiom: ' ... all which, in what follows, is said about Hebraism and Hellenism, has for its main result to show how our Puritans, ancient and modern, have not enough added to their care for walking staunchly by the best light they have, a care that that light be not darkness; how they have developed one side of their humanity at the expense of all others, and have become incomplete and mutilated men in consequence', (*Culture and Anarchy*, 11). This sense that the Puritan ethos was somehow immoderate and led to one-sided development seems to have been a common theme in nineteenth-century Britain. It was also part and parcel of the effort of a growing few to disentangle ethics from theology through the elaboration of a naturalized ideal of human life and virtue.

The intellectual roots of 'internal culture', however, certainly depend upon the Christian emphasis on the inner life over the inauthentic and often immoral compromises forced upon us by social life. For the eighteenth-century rejection of the outward manners of 'fashionable London' by Christians, see Michael Curtin, 'A Question of Manners: Status and Gender in Etiquette and Courtesy', *Journal of Modern History* 57 (September 1985): 395–423.

69. Mill, *Collected Works*, XXI:253.
70. Ibid.
71. Mill, *Collected Works*, X:39.
72. Mill, *Collected Works*, X:230.
73. Mill, *Collected Works*, X:92.
74. Ibid.
75. Mill, *Collected Works*, XX:133.
76. Mill, *Collected Works*, XX:134.
77. Mill, *Collected Works*, XX:134–5, italics added.
78. Mill, *Collected Works*, XX:136.

3

Narrative, Imagination, and the Religion of Humanity in Mill's Ethics

For many of the Benthamite 'philosophic radicals' of the late eighteenth and early nineteenth centuries, Christianity was an especially pernicious superstition. In addition to having a variety of metaphysical and epistemological objections, they also harboured ethical ones. Christianity fostered indifference or outright hostility to human happiness, the keystone of utilitarian morality. Moreover, religious sanctions (e.g. the prospect of eternal damnation or eternal reward) impeded social and political reform – the Church thereby set itself in alliance with the privileged classes to limit the power of the masses.[1]

John Stuart Mill's stance towards religion remained similarly critical throughout his life.[2] Though he argues in his essay 'Theism' that one can justify the possibility of a God using an argument from design, he repudiates the evidence of revelation and the typical Christian conceptions of that God as all-powerful and perfectly benevolent. Further, in 'Utility of Religion' he contends that Christianity weakens the intellect by asking its adherents to accept its flawed theology, fosters selfishness for the majority with its doctrine of heaven and hell, and places questionable moral exemplars before its believers, including a God who seems to act arbitrarily by keeping grace from the millions who lived and died without ever hearing of Christ.[3]

Nevertheless, unlike Bentham and many of his followers, Mill took religion as meeting, however imperfectly, genuine ethical needs. Religion supplies 'ideal conceptions grander and more beautiful than we see realized in the prose of human life', thereby elevating our feelings and acting as a source of personal satisfaction.[4] For nobler spirits inspired by religion's ideals rather than by its sanctions, religion imbues even the smallest of life's activities with a sense of purpose, while also generating greater recognition of duties to others.

Interest in religion's ethical importance was closely interwoven in this period with concern about the negative impact of changes in economic and social life on the British people. This concern was not merely a product of overactive poetic or critical imaginations. Though historians have debated the aptness of the term 'Industrial Revolution' and wondered whether there was, in fact, more continuity than discontinuity between the early eighteenth century and 1780–1850, some changes were clearly significant. First and foremost, there was rapid urbanization. The population of England and Wales doubled between 1780 and 1830, and that increased population was more and more commonly found in cities.[5] There was a fall in rural population in Britain from 71 per cent in 1821 to 56 per cent in 1851,[6] and this was a nation that, at the end of the eighteenth century, was already twice as urbanized as France.[7] In addition, by 1870 the percentage of labour in agriculture had dropped to 22.7 per cent, half of what it had been in 1780, and a figure not reached in the US until the 1920s and in Germany until the 1950s.[8] Relative to other nations, therefore, it was clear that large changes were taking place. Moreover, though there was a moderate increase in real wages and GDP per capita, there was also between 1830 and 1850 a decrease in life expectancy, an increase in infant mortality, and a decrease in average height, which is an indicator of overall health.[9]

Mill shared the unease of many prominent intellectuals of the early to mid nineteenth century, who witnessed the alteration of British life with increasing alarm, especially the transformation of a quiet, predominantly agrarian nation into one on the verge of urban, industrial modernity, and who saw that alteration as having a detrimental impact on the moral health of the nation. Carlyle helped to crystallize resistance to industrialization with his famous rallying cry: 'We have profoundly forgotten everywhere that *Cash-payment* is not the sole relation of human beings.'[10] Coleridge lamented 'the decrease in our feelings of reverence towards mankind at large'.[11] Both men express apprehension about the meaning of the individual life – what can such a life be in a world emptied of reverence, a machine age, in which self-interest grounds interactions with our fellows?

Though Mill consistently holds that 'civilization is a good, that it is the cause of much good, and not incompatible with any', he, along with Carlyle, Coleridge and others, finds many of the moral and political effects of industrialization troubling and needing remedy.[12] He thinks that there are strong tendencies in modern British society which inhibit regard for others and diminish individual happiness. These themes are hit upon again and again throughout his career. From his 1840 essay on Toqueville, for example, one finds the following:

> The private money-getting occupation of almost every one is more or less a mechanical routine; it brings but few of his faculties into action, while its exclusive pursuit tends to fasten his attention and interest exclusively upon himself, and upon his family as an appendage of himself; making him indifferent to the public, to the more generous objects and the nobler interests, and, in his inordinate regard for his personal comforts, selfish and cowardly.[13]

And in his *Autobiography*, Mill decries 'the low moral tone of what in England, is called society; the habit of, not indeed professing, but taking for granted in every mode of implication, that conduct is of course always directed towards low and petty objects'.[14]

This prevalence of self-regard is, of course, a topic of special concern for utilitarians, even as it is a concern shared by others in the period – Mandelbaum argues that the age 'saw its chief moral problem as the problem of extending the bounds of sympathetic, altruistic action'.[15] In Chapter 3 of *Utilitarianism*, Mill argues that the moral feelings would appear arbitrarily associated with the duties specified by the principle of utility unless there was a 'powerful class of sentiments' to ground the association. This basis is the social feelings of mankind – 'the desire to be in unity with our fellow creatures'. These social feelings need nurturing, especially when they are opposed by the forces in industrial society.

It is not, however, only because inordinate self-regard leads to a lack of caring action towards others that it needs to be overcome. It also limits the happiness that the individual himself can enjoy. A passage from *Utilitarianism* captures the threat that stunted fellow-feeling and a 'low' or 'small' conception of our own lives represents for personal happiness:

> When people who are tolerably fortunate in their outward lot do not find in life sufficient enjoyment to make it valuable to them, the cause generally is caring for nobody but themselves. To those who have neither public nor private affections, the excitements of life are much curtailed, and in any case dwindle in value as the time approaches when all selfish interests must be terminated by death; while those who leave after them objects of personal affection, and especially those

who have also cultivated a fellow-feeling with the collective interests of mankind, retain as lively an interest in life on the eve of death as in the vigor of youth and health.[16]

Though Mill is in substantial accord with Carlyle, Coleridge and others on the problems at hand, he can countenance neither of the two most popular alternatives for dealing with those problems, namely calls for a rededication to Christianity (which he takes as exacerbating the problem of self-regard for all but the best people) and efforts to reinstitute more 'traditional' ways of life.[17] Mill is thereby left with the following difficulty: How can one retain the ethical benefits offered by religion without accepting traditional religion or reverting to a reactionary social policy? Mill (again, unlike Bentham) takes the solution to this problem to be vitally important for both the happiness of individuals and for the viability of utilitarian morality.

In this chapter, I shall be emphasizing Mill's responses to this problem that depend on cultivating various propensities of *imagination* – propensities to situate one's life and actions in certain kinds of motivating narratives about ourselves. Other responses to this problem are more directly institutional: reform of workplace, university, family and political life, for example. These will be dealt with more fully in subsequent chapters.

Inspired by Comte, Mill finds great promise in the odd idea of a Religion of Humanity, in which an idealized humanity becomes an object of reverence and in which the morally useful features of traditional religion are supposedly purified and accentuated. This chapter will show how the ethical benefits of the Religion of Humanity – a life imbued with purpose, an improved regard for others, and greater happiness for oneself from the pleasures of fellow-feeling – were to be actualized through the imagination's creation of compelling narratives about humanity. For Mill, the moral psychology of utilitarianism depends upon individuals integrating the narratives that constitute the Religion of Humanity into their self-conceptions. Understanding the ethical importance of the Religion of Humanity therefore implies understanding the central role of imagination in Millian ethical life.[18] This investigation serves to articulate a feature of Mill's utilitarianism that differentiates it from Bentham's, namely his commitment to the importance of a religious sensibility in the moral agent. It also raises the broader philosophical issue of what narratives a psychologically tenable humanist world-view requires – an issue of pressing importance given the growing centrality of conflict between ethical universalism and religious and nationalistic identities.

I shall begin by showing how Comte, whom Mill follows, emphasizes art's role in the idealization of humanity, thereby making humanity worthy of reverence.[19] Mill suggests, however, that idealization is not sufficient for situating the individual in proper relation to humanity. The latter requires imaginatively placing humanity within a drama (i.e. the drama of human history), which has a destination or point, namely the victory of good over evil. The individual is thereby able to describe herself as working in conjunction with others for the triumph of good (i.e. the well-being and perfection of humanity).

In order better to appreciate this seemingly elaborate ethical use of the imagination, it is helpful to contrast it with the views favoured by Mill's fellow utilitarians. Thus, we will go on to look at Bentham's general suspicion of the ethical value of the imagination.

Before concluding, I shall show how Mill attempted to solve the problems raised by Bentham's attack on ethical uses of the imagination. Mill's efforts to defend the imagination by arguing for a realm in which the attribution of truth and falsity is mistaken – and by suggesting that in such cases there can be ethical justifications for the products of imagination – indicate interesting parallels with Kant's postulates.

Imagination, art, and the drama of idealized humanity

Commentators on Mill have often ignored or dismissed outright his discussions of the Religion of Humanity in order to get to his 'serious' moral philosophy. It is useful to ask what led Mill to emphasize this religion, especially since it is often the strangest parts of a thinker's views that provide the most insight. Why did he take this religion to be worth our attention?

In 'Utility of Religion', Mill identifies the value of religion for the individual. It derives from religion's capacity to meet one of our basic needs, a 'craving for higher things'.[20] This craving originates in the recognition that this world, in which one finds suffering, injustice and human relations constituted by 'cash payment', is impoverished and badly flawed. We are prone, therefore, to entertain hopes for something better: 'Belief in a God or Gods, and in a life after death, becomes the canvas which every mind, according to its capacity, covers with such ideal pictures as it can either invent or copy. In that other life each hopes to find the good which he has failed to find on earth, or the better which is suggested to him by the good which on earth he has partially seen and known.'[21] Religion relies on the power of imagination to offer ideal pictures of another world which serve to satisfy us that this imperfect world is not the only one which we can inhabit.

Mill goes on to suggest, however, that our craving for something better need not depend upon satisfaction from an afterlife or heaven. A poetic attitude takes us beyond 'the prose of human life' through beautification of *this* world, thereby providing an attractive alternative to religion:

> The value, therefore, of religion to the individual both in the past and present, as a source of personal satisfaction and of elevated feelings, is not to be disputed. But it still has to be considered, whether in order to obtain this good, it is necessary to travel beyond the boundaries of the world which we inhabit; or whether the idealization of our earthly life, the cultivation of a high conception of what *it* may be made, is not capable of supplying a poetry, and, in the best sense of the word, a religion, equally fitted to exalt the feelings, and (with the same aid from education) still better calculated to ennoble the conduct, than any belief respecting the unseen powers.[22]

Mill anticipates objections to his substitution of a humanist, this-worldly stance for a religious one. First of all, why call it a religion? Mill insists that one can count the Religion of Humanity as a religion even though it involves no belief in God. It meets the two criteria for being a religion, because it has 1) a *creed* (one thinks of the love of humanity or the principle of utility here) that claims authority over the whole of human life – 'a set of beliefs respecting human destiny and duty, to which the believer inwardly acknowledges that all his actions ought to be subordinate', and 2) a *sentiment* connected with this creed which motivates us to live in accordance with it. Mill also notes that 'it is a great advantage ... that this sentiment should crystallize ... round a concrete object; if possible a really existing one, though, in all the more important cases, only ideally present'.[23] Humanity, then, is that concrete/ideally present object, which acts as a locus for generating feelings.

Another objection: Wouldn't it be that 'the small duration, the smallness and insignificance of life, if there is no prolongation of it beyond what we see, makes it impossible that great and elevated feelings can connect themselves with anything laid out on so small a scale'?[24] In other words, wouldn't our earthly existence, emptied of traditional theological import, weigh down even the most fertile imagination and fail to genuinely satisfy our craving for higher things? From a large enough perspective, the individual will always appear miniscule, unimportant and horribly unpoetic.

Mill responds by contending, in partial agreement with the objectors, that in order to find something to satisfy our aspirations, we cannot depend upon the *single* human life. Lives end, and our awareness of death invariably destroys the aesthetically and ethically charged associations we might build around one life, unless we come to see that life as part of something larger which will continue on. But rather than turn to God's providence for a meaningful context for the individual life, as Christians do, or to nature, as the Romantics do, Mill draws our attention to humanity at large: 'Let it be remembered that if individual life is short, the life of the human species is not short; its indefinite duration is practically equivalent to endlessness; and being combined with indefinite capability of improvement, it offers to the imagination and sympathies a large enough object to satisfy any reasonable demand for grandeur of aspiration.'[25]

Thus, the problem that leads Mill to the idea of a Religion of Humanity can be understood as follows. Traditional religion is morally repugnant. Nevertheless, Mill takes religion to be meeting genuine human needs. In order to serve those needs without relying on traditional religion, he recommends idealizing earthly life. But the scope of a single life is not robust enough to sustain this idealization; it requires connecting the individual life to something beyond itself, namely humanity.

The question naturally arises at this point: What kind of picture of humanity should be inculcated in the imagination to make it motivating to us? What kinds of narratives are relevant?

First of all, a basic problem for the attempt to make of humanity a new God and to secure the relation of the individual to it is that it is not readily apparent that humanity can or should generate feelings of veneration. Humanity can seem, in fact, to be a rather unlovely thing. War, evils (both extraordinary and banal), pettiness, selfishness: the catalogue of ugliness goes on and on. One could easily argue that seeing 'humanity' in others is rather unpleasant and hardly productive of feelings of solidarity.

Mill takes his lead here from Comte, who recognizes that humanity needs to be *idealized* by the powers of imagination and art. In *A General View of Positivism*, Comte shows how the imagination's idealization makes out of humanity an object worthy of veneration, thereby prompting the individual to understand himself and others as part of something greater, rather than as mere self-regarding individuals. It is the poet who serves to transform our conception of our individual life: 'The poet is now called to his true mission, which is to give beauty and grandeur to human life, by inspiring a deeper sense of our relation to Humanity.'[26]

Art is defined 'as an ideal representation of Fact' whose object 'is to cultivate our sense of perfection'.[27] By surpassing reality, art stimulates us to amend it.[28] 'Its function is to construct types of the noblest kind, by the contemplation of which our feelings and thoughts may be elevated.'[29]

The power of artistic imagination achieves the substitution of the Religion of Humanity for traditional religion by limiting what is included within the idea of humanity. Comte suggests elsewhere that humanity does not comprise everyone who ever existed, but 'those only who are really capable of assimilation, in virtue of a real co-operation on their part in furthering the common good'.[30] The imagination acts selectively on the real to present something better than the real, thereby directing our moral attention to the ennobling instead of the degrading.

Mill describes this idealization in an essay on Comte:

That the ennobling power of this grand conception may have its full efficacy, we should, with M. Comte, regard the Grand Etre, Humanity, or Mankind, as composed, in the past, solely of those who, in every age and variety of position, have played their part worthily in life. It is only as thus restricted that the aggregate of our species becomes an object deserving our veneration. The unworthy members of it are best dismissed from our habitual thoughts; and the imperfections which adhered through life, even to those of the dead who deserve honorable remembrance, should be no further borne in mind than is necessary not to falsify our conception of facts.[31]

This Comtean theme – artistic imagination as idealizing humanity into an object of veneration, suitable for replacing a traditional notion of God – is appropriated and adapted by Mill. However, for the Religion of Humanity to have its desired effects, the new 'God' that it offers cannot be beautiful and yet distant. A poetic idealization of humanity alone would be insufficient to improve attitudes and conduct.

The image of humanity that Mill paints has two primary characteristics which address this shortcoming. In this image, humanity 1) participates in an epic or drama which 2) has a destination that can be characterized as a Manichean triumph of good over evil. This picture of humanity is meant to draw the individual into identification with it, such that the narrative of the individual's life begins to incorporate and become a part of the story of humanity as a whole. We become characters – we have parts – in humanity's drama. Both Comte and Mill took this to be a significant advantage of humanity over God as an object of worship – humanity needs our participation and help, whereas an omnipotent God presumably needs nothing from us.

By placing humanity within an epic or drama, Mill moves beyond a static idealization into a dynamic one. In so doing he provides narrative structure for humanity and situates it within a story of change and progress:

> As M. Comte truly says, the highest minds, even now, live in thought with the great dead, far more than with the living; and, next to the dead, with those ideal human beings yet to come, whom they are never destined to see. If we honour as we ought those who have served mankind in the past, we shall feel that we are also working for those benefactors by serving that to which their lives were devoted. And when reflection, guided by history, has taught us the intimacy of the connexion of every age of humanity with every other, making us see in the earthly destiny of mankind the playing out of a *great drama*, or the action of a *prolonged epic*, all the generations of mankind become indissolubly united into a single image, combining all the power over the mind of the idea of Posterity, with our best feelings towards the living world which surrounds us, and towards the predecessors who have made us what we are.[32]

We should note a number of things about this long passage. First of all, it is through emphasizing humanity's participation in a drama or epic extended over time that we can see humanity as possessing some kind of unity. Humanity begins to appear as a 'corporate being', rather than a simple aggregate of individuals, when one begins to imagine it as having a destiny. In this way it becomes possible to 'live in thought with the great dead' because one's activities, though on the surface very different from those of the admirable people of the past, can be construed as necessary for playing a role in the same drama of humanity. One does not simply speak and do; one has lines and a part.

Next, it is revealing that Mill invokes the metaphors of drama and epic when speaking about the 'Grand Etre' that is the object of worship in the Religion of Humanity. As we have seen, Mill is working to substitute a poetic for a religious mentality by means of a carefully modulated use of the imagination. The cravings met by the drama of traditional Christianity (i.e. the story of Christ and of the activities of a transcendent God) are now to be addressed by a new, humanist drama (i.e. the story of humanity's progress).

The ultimate goals of promoting utilitarian virtue and of ennobling the life of the individual (thereby avoiding the spiritual impoverishment in which self-regard and instrumental, contractual relations with others dominate life) depend upon getting individuals to incorporate their own life narratives into the story of humanity. This is facilitated when one recognizes that there is a *point* to humanity's drama – that the drama has a destination and meaning. As we shall see in more detail, Mill generally presents this point in terms of a Manichean struggle between good and evil played out over the course of history.

This somewhat strange picture of humanity and its religion becomes easier to comprehend when we begin answering the following question: *How is this kind of narrative brought into the imagination?* Four vehicles for the development of our imaginations are particularly important. They are 1) periodical literature/newspapers, 2) the teaching of history, 3) the 'poetical and artistic', and 4) institutional reforms. I will discuss each in turn.

In his 'Guizot's Essays and Lectures on History' (1845), Mill contrasts the English and Continental minds by appeal to 'their respective literatures' and suggests that the higher tone of the Continental mind can be explained by the pervasiveness of the idea of a destination to history:

Certain conceptions of history considered as a whole, some notions of a progressive unfolding of the capabilities of humanity – of a tendency of man and society towards some distant result – of a *destination*, as it were, of humanity – pervade, in its whole extent, the popular literature of

France. Every newspaper, every literary review or magazine, bears witness of such notions. They are always turning up accidentally, when the writer is ostensibly engaged with something else; or showing themselves as a background behind the opinions which he is immediately maintaining. When the writer's mind is not of a high order, these notions are crude and vague; but they are evidentiary of a tone of thought which has prevailed so long among the superior intellects, as to have spread from them to others, and become the general property of the nation.[33]

Continental literature, then, consistently expresses a sense that the story of humanity is one of meaningful – and progressive – change. Given Mill's belief that ideas and intellectuals can be motive forces in history, the presence of this kind of periodical and newspaper writing is important. It cultivates a sensibility of aspiration in the people.

The second means for developing the imagination is the study of history. Mill consistently speaks of history not simply as a theoretical pursuit whose goal is understanding, but as a subject that can cultivate us as ethical beings. He treats it as a form of paideia. An example of this comes from the late 'Inaugural Address'. In outlining the ideals for a university education, Mill suggests that a professor of history has a responsibility to present his subject in a manner that encourages imaginative engagement by the student. The goal is

> to make him [the student] take interest in history not as a mere narrative, but as a chain of causes and effects still unwinding itself before his eyes, and full of momentous consequences to himself and his descendants; the unfolding of a great epic or dramatic action, to terminate in the happiness or misery, the elevation or degradation, of the human race; an unremitting conflict between good and evil powers, of which every act done by any of us, insignificant as we are, forms one of the incidents; a conflict in which even the smallest of us cannot escape from taking part, in which whoever does not help the right side is helping the wrong, and for our share in which, whether it be greater or smaller, and let its actual consequences be visible or in the main invisible, no one of us can escape the responsibility.[34]

Along with providing a mission statement that must make professors of history tremble, this lofty Manichean/Zoroastrian version of history and of the nature of human progress reveals how full-voiced Mill's claims are.[35] The ethical function of this history involves situating the student within a story (not a mere retelling of past events, but a continuing drama or epic).[36] It is the story of an idealized humanity in which we may insert ourselves as protagonists using the imagination, no matter how humble our status in life.[37] In so doing, we come to see others as potential compatriots in a grand project, thereby encouraging a sense of responsibility towards them beyond what justice and the contractual dictate. We also come to identify ourselves with a form of life which takes place on a temporal and communal scale different from that found in the ordinary run of things (i.e. the 'prose of human life'). This promotes a tone of mind imbued with a sense of the world-historical relevance of even the smallest activities. Actions not only originate from nobler motives than they had before, but they are also placed within a very different context (e.g. as serving the goals of humanity rather than merely the goals of the self). It is precisely the kind of spirit which, for Mill and other nineteenth-century intellectuals, is absent from the common English sensibility, and for utilitarian moral reform to be successful, the ethically charged narratives of the Religion of Humanity must begin to permeate the self-narratives of the citizenry.[38]

The third vehicle for cultivating the imagination is what Mill terms the 'poetical and artistic'. This includes not only poetry and the fine arts, but also the 'poetic' aspects of other kinds of writing. Plato, Demosthenes and Tacitus are all given as examples of authors whose poetic writing in history, rhetoric and philosophy 'brings home to us all those aspects of life which take hold of our nature on its unselfish side, and lead us to identify our joy and grief with the good or ill of the system of which we form a part'.[39]

Mill's emphasis on the arts fits very well into a broader debate taking place in the early to mid nineteenth century about the ameliorating effects of the fine arts on the British people. The recent opening of the National Gallery in the early 1820s coincided with greater emphasis placed on the moral utility of museums, parks, monuments and other public places. Such facilities countered the effects of 'gin palaces' and eased political tensions by softening manners and reducing anger. It was therefore taken to be important to increase the number of, and access to, museums and like public spaces.[40]

Lastly, institutional reform (e.g. of the university, workplace, family, political participation) helps to prepare us for the acceptance of the narratives of the Religion of Humanity. It does so through making our habitual employments such that we more clearly see our connection to others. Through, for example, work in industrial cooperatives and interactions in a family built upon basic equality between wife and husband, we are made aware of the ways in which our interests and those of others are the same, or at least not in opposition. This very large topic will be treated in more detail in Chapters 4 and 5.

Bentham's challenge to the ethical use of imagination

Bentham

Mill's advocacy for the Religion of Humanity is also an advocacy for the ethical importance of the imagination. That religion is effective only insofar as the imagination can generate the kind of narrative we have just outlined. Interestingly, this position on the ethical value of the imagination developed out of an intellectual environment which was quite hostile to the imagination's ethical claims. Bentham's and the early (mid 1820s) Benthamite *Westminster Reviewers'* anti-aestheticism reflects a fundamental suspicion of the imagination.[41] Though Bentham's views on the imagination and art have often been taken as a somewhat humorous example of his eccentricity, they pose a serious challenge to Mill.

Putting aside Mill's apologetics, Thomas contends that the *Westminster* utilitarians were of the mind that the arts should be measured using the rulers of truth and utility:

John Mill later wrote as if the popular notion of a Benthamite as an enemy of poetry derived from a single sentence in an article, by Peregrine Bingham on the poet Thomas Moore, whom Bingham had called 'a poet, and therefore ... *not* a reasoner'. Actually the *Westminster* attacked imaginative literature on a much wider front than this implies. Its writers showed a puritanical dislike of any literature which set out to entertain and amuse. Poetry was tried by a severe utilitarian test.[42]

The utilitarians expected that good art would either produce pleasure or would have to be appropriately didactic if it pretended to serve any positive function at all. In the latter case, it would instruct the reader (the arts of greatest concern were literary) and promote their acceptance of

scientific truth and of the principle of utility. Art's persistent casting off of
these shackles made it an object of deep suspicion among those associated
with the *Westminster*. From their point of view, the mere deviation by these
works of art from treatise form did not imply that new means of evaluation were called for. One genre is as susceptible to judgements of truth
and falsity as any other genre, and must rise to that standard.

Any writing of the period claiming to be a criticism of the *Westminster*
and of Bentham seemed to abide by an unspoken rule that it must expose
their disgraceful philistinism. Hazlitt, Macaulay and Carlyle all found
time for more than one version of this attack. Dickens and Arnold gave it
succour through the century. The radicals' position elicited accusations of
inhumanity, coldness and lack of respect for the sacred and venerable.[43]

The cadre of people who were associated with the new review had
good reason to be suspicious of the imagination, however. For Bentham,
whose overriding focus is on improving our everyday existence – our
day-to-day experience of pleasures and pains – and who has a very
pragmatic and unromantic view of human life, a basic problem with the
imagination is that it can veil the truth about how the features of actions
or states of affairs contribute to well-being. It acts to confound reform by,
among other things, hiding the insidious workings of class and religious
interests behind a curtain of tradition. As Bentham had begun to show
50 years earlier in his *Fragment on Government*, and continued to demonstrate through the time during which the *Westminster Review* was founded,
the imagination is responsible for propping up injustice.[44] It frequently
acts to distort judgements of value, by making some pleasures or pains
seem more or less important than they really are (e.g. aristocrats' playing
down the sufferings of the poor). Rather than indulging the imagination
through the arts, we need to tame it through the disciplined use of reason,
which helps us to recognize what really moves people and to see which
consequences tend to result from which actions. The imagination is more
often than not a luxury of the powerful that the powerless can ill afford,
because the stories which the imagination is likely to tell will rarely be
reformist ones.

Illustrative examples of how the imagination could be employed by
the forces of reaction can be found in the attacks on industrial society by
various poets and critics throughout the nineteenth century, including
Wordsworth, Coleridge, Carlyle and Ruskin. A fascinating exempli-
fication of this comes from a book written by Southey, one that Mill

calls 'the gloomiest book ever written by a cheerful man'.[45] Entitled *Sir Thomas More; or, Colloquies on the Progress and Prospects of Society*, it assaults the 'manufacturing system' using a peculiar narrative technique: More accompanies the narrator on a tour of England that contrasts the new world of manufacturing to the old agrarian, traditional England – to the detriment of the former, of course (Southey is not alone in the use of this kind of comparative practice – Carlyle in *Past and Present* contrasts contemporary England with a twelfth-century monastery).[46] Southey's critique of industrial society comes from the political right, and is part of an aggressive political and social campaign, often finding voice in the *Quarterly Review*, which included such measures as the defence of the landed interests through tariffs on imported grains (Corn Laws). Macaulay, in a biting review of the work, discusses the following section, which, telling as it is, is worth quoting at length:

> We remained a while in silence looking upon the assemblage of dwellings below. Here, and in the adjoining hamlet of Millbeck, the effects of manufactures and of agriculture may be seen and compared. The old cottages are such as the poet and the painter equally delight in beholding. Substantially built of the native stone without mortar, dirtied with no white lime, and their long low roofs covered with slate, if they had been raised by the magic of some indigenous Amphion's music, the materials could not have adjusted themselves more beautifully in accord with the surrounding scene; and time has still further harmonized them with weather stains, lichens, and moss, short grasses, and short fern, and stone-plants of various kinds ... the garden beside, the bee-hives, and the orchard with its bank of daffodils and snowdrops, the earliest and the profusest in these parts, indicate in the owners some portion of ease and leisure, some regard to neatness and comfort, some sense of natural, and innocent, and healthful enjoyment. The new cottages of the manufacturers are upon the manufacturing pattern – naked, and in a row.
>
> 'How is it', said I, 'that everything which is connected with manufactures presents such features of unqualified deformity? From the largest of Mammon's temples down to the poorest hovel in which his helotry are stalled, these edifices have all one character. Time will not mellow them; nature will neither clothe nor conceal them; and they will remain always so offensive to the eye as to the mind.'[47]

Macaulay's response is pithy: 'Mr. Southey has found out a way, he tells us, in which the effects of manufactures and agriculture may be compared. And what is this way? To stand on a hill, to look at a cottage and a factory, and to see which is prettier'.[48] The exchange makes clear what manifestations of imagination and aesthetic sensibility the utilitarians (and as Macaulay demonstrates, some of the Whigs) were fighting against.

This example confronts Mill with a basic problem, however. If, as we have seen, the construction of specific and ethically useful narratives by the imagination is the precondition for the utilitarian agent possessing a 'high tone of mind', then how are we to distinguish between dangerous and desirable performances by the imagination? How can we know if an appeal to imagination such as is made by the Religion of Humanity is inappropriate?

This gets into what we might call the *rhetoric of ethical life* – the uses and abuses of motivating images, metaphors and symbols (e.g. not just for their use in motivating a love for the general good, but also more ordinarily for patriotism, love of family, etc.). More specifically for Mill, this also raises the vexed issue of the relation of utility and truth. Are there times when utility requires lies in order to motivate or for some other reason? Mill clearly wants to avoid that implication.

Mill's reply to the Benthamite challenge

Talk of an idealized humanity and the Manichean drama of its development, therefore, should trigger a Benthamite response to Mill that many twenty-first-century thinkers would second: 'Isn't all this simply false? Isn't all this talk of humanity's history as a drama in which good battles evil just a mere fable?'

Both Comte and Mill believe that reason and imagination can harmonize – they need not be in opposition. Both also support the authority of reason, namely that imagination must give way before evidence. Interestingly, Comte goes beyond Mill in believing that reason gives us access to this new God. Unlike the familiar Christian God, humanity's existence can be established despite Positivism's epistemological demands: 'It must not ... be supposed that the new Supreme Being is, like the old, merely a subjective result of our powers of abstraction. Its existence is revealed to us, on the contrary, by close investigation of objective fact'.[49] Even though humanity's existence is a fact for Comte, it still remains an unmotivating fact without being taken up by art and made beautiful through idealization.

Mill cannot follow Comte down that path. Instead he defends the principle that, when reason is silent – as it is in the case of an idealized humanity – imagination can operate freely of truth as long as it refuses to produce clear falsehood. It remains free to serve ends other than that of truth, including ethical, aesthetic and religious ones, and it does so by making its object more or less attractive to the imaginer. The most thorough treatment of this issue in Mill can be found in the essay 'Utility of Religion' and in the concluding section of 'Theism', the last of his three essays on Religion.

In the final part of 'Theism', after having determined that 'the rational attitude of a thinking mind towards the supernatural, whether in natural or in revealed religion, is that of scepticism as distinguished from belief on the one hand, and from atheism on the other' and that 'there is evidence, but insufficient for proof, and amounting only to one of the lower degrees of probability' for the existence of God, Mill observes that the 'whole domain of the supernatural is thus removed from the region of Belief into that of simple Hope'[50] – that is the supernatural is not amenable to truth claims. This leads to the question 'whether the indulgence of hope, in a region of imagination merely, in which there is no prospect that any probable grounds of expectation will ever be obtained, is irrational, and ought to be discouraged as a departure from the rational principle of regulating our feelings as well as opinions strictly by evidence'.[51] To provide an answer to this, what we need to find are the principles 'which ought to govern the cultivation and the regulation of the imagination', which form a subject that 'has never yet engaged the serious consideration of philosophers, though some opinion on it is implied in almost all modes of thinking on human character and education'.[52]

His conclusion is that the principle which ought to regulate the imagination is that 'literal truth of facts is not the only thing to be considered'.[53] Whether or not, for example, a set of associations is degrading or ennobling should also count for consideration. Associations, in other words, need not only be organized by epistemological principles; they may be in service to ethical or aesthetic principles as well. We should be open to letting the imagination dwell on those possibilities (e.g. a destination for humanity in history) which are the 'most comforting' and the 'most improving', 'without in the least degree overrating the solidity of the grounds for expecting that these rather than any others will be the possibilities actually realized'.[54]

An illustration of this principle is cheerfulness. What is a cheerful disposition, Mill asks, 'but the tendency, either from constitution of habit, to dwell chiefly on the brighter side both of the present and of the future?'[55] Cheerfulness involves, in other words, a selective filtering by the imagination (notice the similarity to the process of idealizing humanity): '(i)f every aspect, whether agreeable or odious of every thing, ought to occupy exactly the same place in our imagination which it fills in fact, and therefore ought to fill in our deliberate reason, what we call a cheerful disposition would be but one of the forms of folly'.[56] The way the cheerful person views the world is not justified epistemically, but ethically.

Mill is quick to point out that cheerfulness need not compromise one's necessary attentiveness to the evils of the world – evils that need to be addressed by good people. But to dwell on the evils of life, or to focus on meanness or baseness, 'makes it scarcely possible to keep up in oneself a high tone of mind'.[57] 'The imagination and feelings become tuned to a lower pitch; degrading instead of elevating associations become connected with the daily objects and incidents of life, and give their colour to the thoughts, just as associations of sensuality do in those who indulge freely in that sort of contemplations.'[58] This is what it means to have one's imagination corrupted. Associations, instead of being directed to the ideal, lead instead to the low and base. By doing so, they fail to meet the need for those 'ideal conceptions grander and more beautiful than we see realized in the prose of human life'.[59]

The key issue, however, is what distinguishes the idealizations of the imagination sanctioned by Mill (e.g. humanity, the world of the cheerful person, etc.) from the idealizations of pre-industrial England provided by Southey, Carlyle and others, or from the idealizations of the relations between the rich and the working classes discussed by Mill in his *Principles of Political Economy*?[60] The feature of cheerfulness just mentioned – that though the cheerful person is attuned to the 'brighter side' of life, he/she is not blind to evil – seems to provide the essential distinction between the appropriate and inappropriate ethical uses of the imagination. The cheerful person retains appreciation for the fact that people can be cruel and do horrible things. If he/she did not retain this understanding, he/she would slip into something like naive optimism, which fails to picture the world in ways accurate enough for the purposes of deliberation and action. [61] The imagination has free rein, in other words, as long as it does not distort the facts of the world necessary for deliberation. Insofar as Southey does that, his vision of traditional English cottages can be ruled out of bounds.

Though the comparison should be drawn with many qualifications, it is fruitful to think of Mill's difficulties here as paralleling the problems which faced Kant and which led him to his postulates of practical reason.[62] For both, ethical life without the resources of traditional religion remains under threat, and a pressing difficulty for the ethicist is to defend ethical life while avoiding theoretically indemonstrable claims. They both, in different ways, eschew theoretical or scientific justifications of their 'postulates' for the sake of ethical or practical ones (while at the same time ruling out various alternatives that make claims which go beyond what experience can justify).

Mill's treatment of this subject is much more ad hoc than Kant's; it attributes importance to religion for moral psychological reasons rather than because practical reason demands it (the postulates act as conditions for the possibility of the highest good); and Kant would, perhaps rightly, claim that Mill's own position is untenable without the rejection of empiricism and the acceptance of the phenomenal/noumenal distinction. Moreover, Kant defends something much more religiously orthodox than does Mill. Nevertheless, given the frequent contrasts drawn between the moral theories of both men, it is revealing to note their similarity in defending the importance of a religious sensibility for ethical life, especially when that defence comes in the face of many – including Bentham, the atheists of the radical French enlightenment and the eighteenth century's version of Spinoza – who denied that very thing.

Conclusion

We best comprehend Mill's emphases on the Religion of Humanity and on the ethical value of imagination when we recognize their importance in constructing a compelling humanist narrative. For Mill, to avoid the malaise and self-regard identified by critics of industrialization requires a capacity to understand life in a manner that transcends the realm of ordinary human transactions. It requires more than science and fact could offer. People like Carlyle and Coleridge understood much better than Bentham and his followers, Mill felt, that humans rarely flourish in a world which, though eminently practical and efficient, finds its ideals in the paltry and profane. This led Carlyle and others, however, into what Mill considered to be an unfortunate religious and metaphysical mysticism. The pressing issue was how to encourage a moral psychology which is suitable to utilitarian morality and to remedying the ills brought on by modernity, without sacrificing the authority of our reason and without reverting back to conservative social policy or a traditional religious position that depends on discredited metaphysical and ethical views. How does one, in other words, encourage caring for others without relying on nostalgia or mystery (a mystery that can easily slide into superstition)?

Mill's hopes rested on the narratives provided by an imagination drawing on the resources of the Religion of Humanity. These narratives act to infuse our world with possibility, with awareness that it could be otherwise (and better). It promotes a new, joyful sense of our lives and our actions as having a relation to the sacred – not because we are the creatures of a transcendent God, but because we are a part of something greater than ourselves, namely an idealized humanity. We can come to see our conduct as in partnership with those ideal figures whom we admire and who have prominent roles in the drama of humanity's historical development. In so doing, we are meant to achieve the 'ideal-ization of our earthly life, the cultivation of a high conception of what *it* may be made'.[63]

The exploration of Mill's views on the Religion of Humanity raises a number of themes that I shall finish this chapter by noting. First, it reveals how the temperament of a thinker can express itself, not just in doctrine, but in overall tone. In this case, we find that some of the most significant differences between Mill and Bentham stem from the presence of a religious sensibility in Mill (e.g. a concern for the high versus the low, and for reverence and the sacred as important features of ethical life), and its almost complete absence in Bentham. In this respect, Bentham is the true heir of Epicurus. He is relentlessly this-worldly.

Secondly, this work brings out Mill's perfectionism (i.e. humans, at a very basic level, can be improved over time), since the Religion of Humanity is part of that overall project of improvement and cultivation. Unlike for other, more sanguine supporters of modernity and the progress of civilization, Mill does not think that this improvement results naturally from the effects of industrialization and growing democracy. We have to *act* to bring it about. This, in turn, depends on the kinds of institutional reforms (especially reform of education) treated here and later in the book.

The political ramifications of this perfectionist bent are significant. Perfectionism of the kind reflected in Mill's programme for the Religion of Humanity brings into political discourse a set of justifications for institutions very foreign to someone of Bentham's camp, namely that institutions can be judged good or bad by their impact on the cultivation of character. In the *Autobiography*, Mill confirms this when he states that, with his early break with Benthamite utilitarianism, he began to see 'the choice of political institutions as a *moral and educational question* more than one of *material interests*, thinking that it ought to be decided mainly by the consideration, what great improvement in life and culture stands next in order for the people concerned, as the condition of their further progress, and what institutions are most likely to promote that'.[64] This kind of statement suggests that the realms of moral perfection and of the exercise of social and political power are not necessarily as well segregated as libertarian readings of *On Liberty* might have us believe.

Lastly, comprehending the Religion of Humanity's place in Mill's thought provides us with a much more concrete sense than Chapter 3 of *Utilitarianism* of what cultivating a utilitarian agent and a 'sense of unity' with others amounts to. This can also be seen in broader terms as a problem for any kind of ethical cosmopolitanism: What can lead us to care for others, whom we may never meet, *as humans* (rather than as fellow-Americans or fellow-lovers of philosophy, etc.)? As strange as the Religion of Humanity may seem, is it simply a relic of nineteenth-century thought or does something like Mill's account underlie contemporary ethical universalism/cosmopolitanism?

A relevant point of comparison here is Rorty's discussion of solidarity in *Contingency, Irony, and Solidarity*. Rorty's basic problem is similar to Mill's. He thinks that there is such a thing as moral progress, and that this progress involves greater feelings of solidarity among humans as humans. This is a difficult goal to achieve, however, because we are more consistently motivated by more parochial forms of identification with others. Rorty uses the example that Jews in Denmark and Italy were more likely than those in Belgium to be helped by their neighbours. He suggests that this is so, not because they were more readily described as 'fellow human beings' in those two countries, but rather because they were more readily seen as 'fellow parents' or 'fellow Bocce players' or 'fellow Milanese'.[65]

How, then, can we expect human solidarity to become more common? Rorty's answer is the following:

> In my utopia, human solidarity would be seen not as a fact to be recognized by clearing away 'prejudice' or burrowing down to previously hidden depths but, rather, as a goal to be achieved. It is to be achieved not by inquiry but by imagination, the imaginative ability to see strange people as fellow sufferers. Solidarity is not discovered by reflection but created. It is created by increasing our sensitivity to the particular details of the pain and humiliation of other, unfamiliar sorts of people.[66]

Rorty rejects solidarity grounded on recognition of a core self or human essence (e.g. rationality). Instead he depends upon the recognition of the pain and humiliation that others suffer as a foundation for identifying with others. Though nothing in Mill's view would rule out the contribution of a shared potential for pain and humiliation as a ground for solidarity, it is interesting to note how different the ground he champions is. One might ask whether the more concrete foundation offered by Rorty – one which has a this-worldly quality which someone like Bentham could readily appreciate – has advantages or disadvantages in relation to the grander narrative of Manichean struggle put forward by Mill, in which the solidarity I feel for another rests on imagining him/her as a fellow-worker trying to further the ends of humanity.[67]

Endnotes

1. For an excellent account of Bentham's views on religion, see James E. Crimmins, *Secular Utilitarianism* (Oxford: Clarendon Press, 1990).
2. Some helpful discussions of Mill on religion include Karl Britton, 'John Stuart Mill on Christianity' in John Robson and Michael Laine, eds, *James and John Stuart Mill: Papers of the Centenary Conference* (Toronto: University of Toronto Press, 1976); Alan Millar, 'Mill on Religion' in John Skorupski, ed., *The Cambridge Companion to Mill* (Cambridge: Cambridge University Press, 1998); Alan Ryan, *J. S. Mill* (London: Routledge & Kegan Paul, 1974); and

Linda Raeder, *John Stuart Mill and the Religion of Humanity* (Columbia, MO: University of Missouri Press, 2002).

3. John Stuart Mill, *The Collected Works of John Stuart Mill*, John M. Robson, gen. ed., 33 vols (Toronto: University of Toronto Press, 1963–91), X:422–5.

4. Mill, *Collected Works*, X:419.

5. Charles H. Feinstein, 'Pessimism Perpetuated: Real Wages and the Standard of Living in Britain during and after the Industrial Revolution', *The Journal of Economic History*, Vol. 58, No. 3 (September 1998), 625–58.

6. From N. F. R. Crafts, 'Some Dimensions of the "Quality of Life" during the British Industrial Revolution', *The Economic History Review*, Vol. 50, No. 4 (November, 1997), 617–39.

7. Nicholas Crafts, 'Forging Ahead and Falling Behind: The Rise and Relative Decline of the First Industrial Nation', *The Journal of Economic Perspectives*, Vol. 12, No. 2 (Spring 1998), 193–210.

8. Crafts, 'Forging Ahead and Falling Behind: The Rise and Relative Decline of the First Industrial Nation', *The Journal of Economic Perspectives*, Vol. 12, No. 2 (Spring 1998), 195.

9. Crafts, 'Some Dimensions of the "Quality of Life" during the British Industrial Revolution', *The Economic History Review*, Vol. 50, No. 4 (November, 1997), 623, 632, 634.

10. Thomas Carlyle, *Past and Present* (London: Ward, Lock and Bowden, Ltd., 1897), 202–3. See also his essay 'Characteristics', where he bemoans the fact that 'Belief, Faith has well-nigh vanished from the world', (from *A Carlyle Reader*, G. B. Tennyson (ed.) (Cambridge: Cambridge University Press, 1984), 91).

11. S. T. C. Coleridge, *On the Constitution of the Church and State According to the Idea of Each (3rd Edition), and Lay Sermons (2nd Edition)* (London: William Pickering, 1839), 279.

12. Mill, *Collected Works*, XVIII:119.

13. Mill, *Collected Works*, XVIII:169. Compare this to what Engels has to say in *The Condition of the Working Class in England* in 1844:

> The very turmoil of the streets has something repulsive, something against which human nature rebels. The hundreds and thousands of all classes and ranks crowding past each other, are they not all human beings with the same qualities and powers, and with the same interest in being happy? And have they not, in the end, to seek happiness in the same way, by the same means? And still they crowd one another, and their only agreement is the tacit one, that each keep to his own side of the pavement, so as not to delay the opposing streams of the crowd, while it occurs to no man to honour another with so much as a glance. The brutal indifference, the unfeeling isolation of each in his private interest

becomes the more repellant and offensive, the more these individuals are crowded together, within a limited space. And, however much one may be aware that this isolation of the individual, this narrow self-seeking is the fundamental principle of our society everywhere, it is nowhere so shamelessly barefaced, so self-conscious as just here in the crowding of the great city. The dissolution of mankind into monads, of which each one has a separate principle, the world of atoms, is here carried out to its utmost extreme.

Excerpt from *Art In Theory, 1815–1900*, Harrison, Wood and Gaiger (eds), Oxford: Blackwell Publishers, 1998, 295.

14. Mill, *Collected Works*, I:61.
15. Maurice Mandelbaum, *History, Man, and Reason* (Baltimore, MD: Johns Hopkins University Press, 1971), 35.
16. Mill, *Collected Works*, X:215.
17. The conservative call for a slower, more traditional society – a call made by, among others, Carlyle, Southey and many of the proponents of the Corn Laws protecting British agriculture and landowners – was heard throughout the early and mid nineteenth century and often took the form of polemics against the new science of political economy and against the industrialism it seemed to promote.
18. The imagination is a sorely understudied topic in Mill's ethics. As an example, the *Cambridge Companion to Mill*'s extensive index includes no references to imagination. Some mention of the imagination in the context of ethics can be found in the following: Lou Matz 'The Utility of Religious Illusion: A Critique of J. S. Mill's Religion of Humanity', *Utilitas* 12 (2000), 137–54; Wendy Donner, *The Liberal Self* (Ithaca, NY: Cornell University Press, 1991), 97–106; John Robson's 'J. S. Mill's Theory of Poetry' in J. B. Schneewind, ed., *Mill: A Collection of Critical Essays* (London: Macmillan, 1968); Robson's *The Improvement of Mankind* (London: University of Toronto Press, 1968); and Susan Feagin, 'Mill and Edwards on the Higher Pleasures', *Philosophy* 58 (1983): 244–52.
19. Comte, however, tended to value the Religion of Humanity as a source of social and political stability, while for Mill it had an important ethical function.
20. Mill, *Collected Works*, X:419.
21. Ibid.
22. Mill, *Collected Works*, X:419–20.
23. Mill, *Collected Works*, X:332–3.
24. Mill, *Collected Works*, X:420.
25. Ibid.

26. Auguste Comte, *A General View of Positivism* (1848) (Dubuque, IA: Brown Reprints, 1971), 368.

27. Comte, 300.

28. Comte, 302.

29. Ibid.

30. As quoted in T. R. Wright, *The Religion of Humanity* (Cambridge: Cambridge University Press, 1986), 23. For another treatment of the Comtean idea of Humanity, see Andrew Wernick, *Auguste Comte and the Religion of Humanity* (Cambridge: Cambridge University Press, 2001), Chapter 7.

31. Mill, *Collected Works*, X:334.

32. Mill, *Collected Works*, X:334, italics added.

33. Mill, *Collected Works*, XX:260–1. See also Mill's essay on Coleridge (X:39), in which he claims that the series of writers and thinkers from Herder to Michelet 'by making the facts and events of the past have a meaning and an intelligible place in the gradual evolution of humanity, have at once given history, even to the imagination, an interest like romance'.

34. Mill, *Collected Works*, XXI:244.

35. This historical Manicheanism should be distinguished from the more metaphysically robust religious Manicheanism, for which the evidence is 'too shadowy and unsubstantial' (*Collected Works*, X:425).

36. Bentham's rejection of ethical function of history is summed up nicely by Winch: ' ... Bentham remained largely indifferent to much that had preoccupied Scottish historians of civil society, the origins of historical development of forms of law and government: he saw some merit in the work of Ferguson and Kames, but history was more often regarded by Bentham not merely as a record of error (what it could also be to Scottish historians), but as a record of *uninstructive* error, constantly in danger of succumbing to the Chinese or Blackstonian disease of ancestor-worship'. See Stefan Collini, Donald Winch and John Burrow, *That Noble Science of Politics: A study in nineteenth-century intellectual history* (Cambridge: Cambridge University Press, 1983), 94.

37. The idea that one may be a protagonist or agent no matter what one's social standing indicates imagination's potential for erasing fundamental class conflict from public life. This has obvious political implications, some of them strongly conservative. For a treatment of this general issue, see Terry Eagleton, *The Ideology of the Aesthetic* (Oxford: Basil Blackwell, 1990). It is useful to note, however, that Mill seems much less concerned about the problems of overcoming class conflict than Matthew Arnold, whose idea of 'culture' grows out of a clear anxiety about class conflict (see Eagleton, 'Sweetness and Light for all', *Times Literary Supplement*, 21 January 2000, 14–15).

38. Though central, this is not the only requirement of utilitarian moral reform. For Mill, unlike for Comte, the Religion of Humanity has *no* institutional structure or associated ritual. This distances it further from traditional Christianity (not simply in the form of a doctrine, but as a set of practices) and from its status as a religion at all (rather than as an ethical ideal, which is how I think it should be understood). It is a religion, in other words, only in name (though the name 'Religion of Humanity' undoubtedly served valuable polemical functions in both France and England by, among other things, provoking opponents). Lacking institutions, the Religion of Humanity's ethical importance is of a largely intellectual and imaginative variety.

    The institutional structures and rituals meant to further the development of utilitarian agents do not come from a humanist religion, but from the economic realm (e.g. the worker cooperatives recommended in the *Principles of Political Economy*) and from civil society (e.g. the family reformed along lines argued for in the *Subjection of Women*). An exhaustive treatment of the Religion of Humanity in Mill would have to examine how the sensibility deriving from the Religion's view of humanity and its history supports such economic and civil institutions, and, perhaps more importantly, how it garners support from them.

    The recognition that Mill's version of the Religion of Humanity lacks an institutional structure brings into question attempts to take this religion as a sign of an anti-liberal tendency in Mill (which may still be there, but which cannot depend on the evidence of his religious views) and efforts to interpret him as supporting a type of civil religion.

39. Mill, *Collected Works*, XXI:254.

40. For a discussion of these points, see Holger Hoock, 'Reforming culture: national art institutions in the age of reform', in *Rethinking the Age of Reform*, Burns and Innes (eds) (Cambridge: Cambridge University Press, 2003), 254–70.

41. The *Westminster Review* was the response of the Radicals to the *Edinburgh Review* (Whig-orientation) and the *Quarterly Review* (Tory-orientation).

42. William Thomas, *The Philosophic Radicals: Nine Studies in Theory and Practice 1817–1841* (Oxford: Clarendon Press, 1979), 161.

43. These same barbs that were tossed at the *Westminster* set had been thrown against the English Jacobins of the late eighteenth century. See Thomas, 163.

44. An example of this is given in Bentham's *An Introduction to the Principles of Morals and Legislation* (Oxford: Clarendon Press, 1996), where he argues that maxims like *Delegatus non potest delegare* and *Fiat Justitia, ruat coelum* are examples of the corrupting power of the imagination. In both of these

cases, the 'music of the maxim, absorbing the whole imagination' drowns 'the cries of humanity along with the dictates of common sense' (22).

45. Mill, *Collected Works*, XXII.229.

46. This emphasis on the medieval and early modern can also be found prominently in the early- to mid-nineteenth-century arts with the Gothic Revival and the Pre-Raphaelite Brotherhood – both of which are influenced to a greater or lesser extent by Ruskin.

47. Robert Southey, *Sir Thomas More: Or Colloquies on the Progress and Prospects of Society*, 2 vols (London: John Murray, 1829), I:173–4.

48. Thomas Macaulay, *Critical and Historical Essays*, 2 vols (London: Everyman's Library, 1937), II:198.

49. Comte, *A General View of Positivism*, 354. Mill's relation to the claim that humanity's existence is an 'objective fact' remains more problematic than Comte's relation, because of Mill's commitment to 'methodological individualism' in the social sciences. The most basic expression of this is his prioritizing of psychology over sociology. Comte's reversal of that priority – his contention that man as a psychological being is derivative from man as a social being – leads him to ascribe greater ontological heft to humanity than to the individual: 'Man indeed, as an individual, cannot properly be said to exist, except in the exaggerated abstractions of modern metaphysicians. Existence in the true sense can only be predicated of Humanity' (354). This view creates problems for Mill's wholehearted acceptance of Comte's Religion of Humanity. Mill cannot acknowledge the ontological status Comte gives to humanity. Since humanity does not have the same status as a 'fact' that it does in Comte's system, Mill must place more stress on the role of imagination. The facts for Mill (as for Bentham) are those of individual human beings (e.g. beliefs, desires, pains, pleasures) – all social facts are reducible to these and explainable by them. For an excellent discussion of these issues, see John Skorupski, *John Stuart Mill* (London: Routledge, 1989), 276.

50. Mill, *Collected Works*, X:482–3.

51. Mill, *Collected Works*, X:483.

52. Ibid.

53. Mill, *Collected Works*, X:485. Replying to Bentham's claim that 'All poetry is misrepresentation', which Mill applies to oratory and popular writing of every kind, he argues that 'Bentham's charge is true to the fullest extent; all writing which undertakes to make men feel truths as well as see them, does take up one point at a time, does seek to impress that, to drive that home, to make it sink into and colour the whole mind of the reader or hearer. It is justified in doing so, if the portion of truth which it thus enforces be that which is called for by the occasion. All writing addressed to the feelings has

a natural tendency to exaggeration; but Bentham should have remembered that in this, as in many things, we must aim at too much, to be assured of doing enough' (Mill, *Collected Works*, X:114).

54. Mill, *Collected Works*, X:483.
55. Mill, *Collected Works*, X:484.
56. Ibid.
57. Mill, *Collected Works*, X:484.
58. Mill, *Collected Works*, X:484–5.
59. Mill, *Collected Works*, X:419.
60. In the *Principles*, Mill states that many of the rich want to be '*in loco parentis* to the poor, guiding and restraining them like children' (Mill, *Collected Works*, III:759). This leads him to the following attack on a particular kind of idealization:

> This is the ideal of the future, in the minds of those whose dissatisfaction with the present assumes the form of affection and regret towards the past. Like other ideals, it exercises an unconscious influence on the opinions and sentiments of numbers who never consciously guide themselves by any ideal. It has also this in common with other ideals, that it has never been historically realized. It makes its appeal to our imaginative sympathies in the character of a restoration of the good times of our forefathers. But no times can be pointed out in which the higher classes of this or any other country performed a part even distantly resembling the one assigned to them in this theory. It is an idealization, grounded on the conduct and character of here and there an individual. All privileged and powerful classes, as such, have used their power in the interest of their own selfishness, and have indulged their self-importance in despising, and not in lovingly caring for, those who were in their estimation, degraded by being under the necessity of working for their benefit.
>
> *Collected Works*, III:759-60

What we should take from this is Mill's continued wariness of the imaginative activity of idealization.

61. The potential lack of conflict between imagination and truth is emphasized by Mill in the *Autobiography* in a discussion of his disputes with Roebuck on the importance of the arts:

> It was in vain I urged on him that the imaginative emotion which an idea, when vividly conceived, excites in us, is not an illusion but a fact, as real as any of the other qualities of objects; and far from implying anything erroneous and delusive in our mental apprehension of the object, is quite consistent with our most accurate knowledge and most perfect practical recognition of all its physical and intellectual laws and relations. The intensest feeling of the beauty of a cloud lighted by the setting sun, is no

hindrance to my knowing that the cloud is vapour of water, subject to all the laws of vapours in a state of suspension; and I am just as likely to allow for, and act on, these physical laws whenever there is occasion to do so, as if I had been incapable of perceiving any distinction between beauty and ugliness.

Collected Works, I:157

62. For Kant's discussion of the postulates, see the *Critique of Practical Reason* (5:122ff). Section 87 in the *Critique of Judgement* is also pertinent, especially his account of the moral problems faced by the righteous man (he uses Spinoza as an example) who reveres the moral law but does not believe in God (5:452–3).

63. Mill, *Collected Works*, X:420.

64. Mill, *Collected Works*, I:177.

65. Richard Rorty, *Contingency, Irony, and Solidarity* (Cambridge: Cambridge University Press, 1989), 189–91.

66. Ibid, xvi.

4

Social and Political Dimensions of Aesthetic Education: Family, Marriage and Gender Relations

Introduction

Up to this point, I have reconstructed the debates which led Mill to emphasize aesthetic education, and made the desiderata of such an education – cultivated feelings and noble imaginings – more determinate and open to philosophical analysis, in order to provide a richer context for understanding Mill's conceptions of character and character education. Mill's halting efforts open up new horizons of concern for character and represent one of his main attempts to incorporate some of the ideas of, among others, Coleridge, Carlyle and the Germans, while revising and rejecting parts of his Benthamite inheritance, particularly those sceptical and anti-perfectionist tendencies shared with thinkers like Macaulay.

In this chapter and the next, I shall give more attention to the institutional mechanisms or means whereby one is given an aesthetic education. The point of doing so is to go further beyond the mere articulation of ideals for character development to recognition of the spirit or texture of a Millian life, that is, how this life gets fostered and sustained over time by our everyday pursuits. This moves us away from a merely static conception of ideal character types to a vivid realization of what a good life amounts to and how it is built out of daily activity. It makes Mill's vision more readily available to our moral imaginations, such that we can better appreciate what this life looks like in the concrete.

Through reasonably broad reading in Mill's corpus it becomes clear that the mechanisms for creation of affective and imaginative propensities depend a great deal upon institutional structures. Aesthetic education, therefore, must be seen in the context of Mill's writings on institutions (and, as an additional benefit, his writings on institutions profit from being read through the lens of aesthetic education). The character development indicated by 'aesthetic education', though it may produce 'beauty' of character, often does so through very ordinary causes, such as the way in which chores are distributed in a home or how workers make decisions in the workplace. This chapter and the next will examine, for reasons to be canvassed in a moment, the impact of family and workplace on character.

Mill is not alone in emphasizing the relation between cultivation and institutions. Coleridge, as Raymond Williams notes, influenced Mill by placing special weight on cultivation as a social idea: ' ... for Mill it was Coleridge who first attempted to define, in terms of his changing society, the *social* conditions of man's perfection. Coleridge's emphasis in his social writings is on *institutions*. The promptings to perfection came indeed from "the cultivated heart"—that is to say, from man's inward consciousness—but, as Burke before him, Coleridge insisted on man's need for institutions which should confirm and constitute his personal efforts. Cultivation, in fact, though an inward was never a merely individual process.'[1] The cultivation of the feelings and the imagination depends not only on my experience with the arts or with poetic forms of history and philosophy, but also on whether the institutions which structure most of my day and my conduct contribute to or counteract that cultivation. The causes of aesthetic education are badly misconstrued if they are seen only in terms of largely solitary, intentional activities.

This chapter and the next will reveal, therefore, how closely tied Mill's ethics are to his projects for social and political reform. In the first place, we cannot fully appreciate his ethical views without reference to his writings on society. And though social and political progress never reduces to progress in character education – progress in justice and material well-being are also essential components – the cultivation of our humanity is never far removed from political and social debate in Mill's texts or in the period as a whole.[2] My goal here, then, is to bring works like the *Subjection of Women* and *Principles of Political Economy* into the narrative of aesthetic education, in order to enrich the latter and to give us a new way of looking at the former.

We shall be looking at how inequality in the family and the opposition of interests (coupled with inequalities) in the workplace shape character development. These are the basic principles of family and work that Mill wants to reform. Making the case for reform depends on his ability to show how inequality and opposition of interests cause undesirable character dispositions, including most prominently a lack of capacity for affectionate, sympathetic bonds with others (e.g. feelings of love, solidarity, tenderness, etc.) and a cramped moral imagination.

But why does Mill think institutions have any causal influence on character? His answer to this can be brought out by a passage from his second essay on Tocqueville [1840]: 'It has often been said, and requires to be repeated still oftener, that books and discourses alone are not education; that life is a problem, not a theorem; that action can only be learnt in action. A child learns to write its name only by a succession of trials; and is a man to be taught to use his mind and guide his conduct by mere precept? What can be learnt in schools is important, but not all-important. The main branch of the education of human beings is their habitual employment.'[3] Since Mill goes on to say that our habitual employment is structured by institutions, the connection of education to institutions is clear.

Among those institutions most important for their effect on character, family and workplace are particularly significant institutions for two reasons. First, Mill consistently speaks of the family and the workplace as 'schools' – schools of sympathy, of moral development, and of virtues. They thereby do more than fulfil specified social functions (e.g. keeping social order, distributing wealth); they educate and shape the individuals who participate in them.

Second, the family and the workplace are the paradigmatic modern institutions, as civil society and family gain in importance vis-à-vis political society. In opposition to the emphases of some earlier theorists, Mill downplays the importance of political institutions for modernity. It may be the case that '(c)itizenship, in free countries, is partly a school of society in equality; but', Mill goes on, 'citizenship fills only a small place in modern life, and does not come near the daily habits or inmost sentiments. The family, justly constituted, would be the real school of the virtues of freedom.'[4] Similar claims about the workplace, which we shall review in the next chapter, are made in Mill's economic writings.

A telling indicator of the importance of family and workplace for cultivation of feeling and imagination can be found in Mill's treatment of history and historical method. It is the 'subjective historian' like Michelet, not the traditional historian of political life, who goes beyond telling us 'how mankind acted at each period' to comprehending 'how they felt', giving us the spirit of the age rather than its 'dry husk'.[5] Those in danger of supplying only the dry husk are those who ignore institutions like family and workplace in favour of looking at political institutions, because it is the former that can claim responsibility for shaping how humanity 'felt'. Mill's critique of Niebuhr's historical work on Rome is worth quoting in full at this point:

> But without meaning disparagement to Niebuhr, it has always struck us as remarkable, that a mind so fitted to throw light upon the dark places in the Roman manner of existence, should have exhausted its efforts in clearing up and rendering intelligible the merely civic life of the Roman people. By the aid of Niebuhr, we now know, better than we had ever reckoned upon knowing, what the Roman republic was. But what the Romans themselves were, we scarcely know better than we did before. It is true that citizenship, its ideas, feelings, and active duties, filled a larger space in ancient, than in any form of modern life; but they did not constitute the whole. A Roman citizen had a religion and gods, had a religious morality, had domestic relations; there were women in Rome as well as men; there were children, who were brought up and educated in a certain manner; there were, even in the earliest period of the Roman commonwealth, slaves. Of all this, one perceives hardly anything in Niebuhr's voluminous work. The central idea of the Roman religion and polity, the family, scarcely shows itself, except in connexion with the classification of the citizens; nor are we made to perceive in what the beliefs and modes of conduct of the Romans, respecting things in general, agreed, and in what disagreed, with those of the rest of the ancient world. Yet the mystery of the Romans and their fortunes must lie there.[6]

What the 'Roman manner of existence' was and what the 'Romans themselves were' – in other words, what the interior life of the Roman was like – can only be gleaned from looking at the Roman family. This, as Mill suggests, is even more applicable to modern people, and reflects the causal importance of institutions like the family in shaping our interiority. It is to the dynamics of these institutions, and to their effects on character education in the guise of aesthetic education, that we now turn.

The Family

The radical nature of Mill's feminism and of his call for equality between men and women is often lost to us. This is especially true because, as with *On Liberty*, the subsequent success of the views that Mill espouses have made *The Subjection of Women* and his other writings on gender seem only mildly interesting. A brief sketch of the relevant Victorian legal, scientific and social attitudes towards women and marriage helps to rectify that problem.

The legal status of married women in nineteenth-century Britain reflected a subordination of the wife to the husband. This subordination is indicated by the following: 1) women had fewer grounds for divorce than men until 1923;[7] 2) husbands absolutely controlled their wives personal property (with the occasional exception of land) until the Married Women's Property Acts of 1870 and 1882;[8] 3) children were the husband's; 4) rape was impossible within a marriage; and 5) the wife lacked legal personhood, since the husband represented her (thereby eliminating the need for women's suffrage). The lack of legal personhood for the wife grew out of the principle of 'spousal unity', which had its origins in the book of Genesis' notion that 'a man leaves his father and his mother and clings to his wife, and they become one flesh' (Genesis 3:24). Blackstone shows the influence of this idea on English common law when he remarks that 'by marriage, the husband and wife are one person in law'.[9]

The legal position of women got support from a variety of theological and scientific claims about women and their capacities. For example, many of the greatest British scientific minds of the mid- to late-nineteenth century, including Spencer, Darwin, Galton and Huxley, asserted the inferiority of women. Darwin claims in the *Descent of Man* (1871) that 'it is generally admitted that with women the powers of intuition, of rapid perception, and perhaps of imitation, are more strongly marked than in man; but some, at least, of these faculties are characteristic of the lower races, and therefore of a past and lower state of civilization'.[10]

Socially, there was a growing idealization of the wife as, in the title of Coventry Patmore's poem of 1854, 'The Angel in the House'. Though a number of historians have rightly questioned the extent to which this ideal of domesticity and feminine virtue was actually realized, the ideal was certainly widespread and exerted some psychic force on both men and women.[11] The back-handed compliments of women as better and kinder than men – compliments that Mill condemned as hypocritical and as facilitating the inequality of women – reflect the way in which women were associated with the home and how they were taken to act as a bulwark against the rough-and-tumble outside world.

In this broader context, one can discern the radicalism in advocating for a marriage between equals – a companionate rather than a patriarchal vision of married life.[12] To many, the idea that marriage could be a relation between equals and friends was taken as unrealistic and threatening to the established order. The value of a friendship of equals between husband and wife is Mill's most basic normative commitment in *The Subjection of Women*. As he contends during a vigorous debate with Comte about the nature of women, any marriage without such a friendship is an impoverished one: 'Without any empty sentimentality, I find that the affection a person of a somewhat elevated nature may feel for another being who is subject to his authority is always somewhat imperfect, acceptable only because one cannot feel more complete sympathy for another.'[13] He later claims in his 1854 diary that this best form of marriage is open only to the 'high-minded', since 'it is only the high-minded to whom equality is really agreeable. A proof is that they are the only persons who are capable of strong and durable attachments to their equals; while strong and durable attachments to superiors or inferiors are far more common and are possible to the vulgarest natures.'[14]

The Subjection of Women begins with the object of the essay, which is to show: 'That the principle which regulates the existing social relations between the two sexes—the legal subordination of one sex to the other—is wrong in itself, and now one of the chief hindrances to human improvement; and that it ought to be replaced by a principle of perfect equality, admitting no power or privilege on the one side, nor disability on the other.'[15] As we go along, we will see Mill offering an account of how the affections and imagination squeeze into the moulds provided for them, how malformation of those features of the self arises out of inequality, and how this malformation counteracts the desiderata of aesthetic education as previously discussed (e.g. the promotion of higher pleasures and non-self-interested passions, and a conception of oneself as linked to something great and noble).

Mill's discussions of equality can come across to contemporary ears as banal. Advocacy for equality is like advocacy for world peace. At the time, however, his recommendations were extremely controversial (as they might be today, on reflection, if their full implications were taken seriously). Moreover, his interest in equality is not simply an interest in general claims of justice; it is an interest in how inequality (of power, of authority, of agency, of social status) impacts the character of those who 'benefit' by it and of those who are subject to it. Mill wants to present images of the kinds of men and women created by the current state of the home, while providing a believable account of *how* this creation comes about.

In showing that equality should govern the 'social relations between the two sexes', Mill must defend against two preliminary objections: 1) that social life will collapse into anarchy if relations are made more equal; and 2) that women are not capable of being fundamentally different from how they already are.

The response to the first objection had to relax fears created by the Terror and by the many succeeding years of commentary on it. One of Mill's remarks to Comte makes this clear. Mill, while advocating equality between the sexes, is very careful to 'reject with all my strength of mind the anarchical doctrine of revolutionary times, which openly contradicts the whole of human experience'.[16] The rejection of the anarchical equality of the Revolutionary period put the burden of proof on reformers to show, as Mill puts it, how 'equality' can be compatible with '[social] harmony'.

The answer to this challenge depends on social statics, or 'the science which ascertains the conditions of stability in the social union'.[17] Social statics articulates the conditions for the existence of various social facts (e.g. 'stable political union') by looking at the necessary relations which exist between the facts (e.g. between a society's 'state of civilization' and its 'form of government').[18] Those who defended inequality in the family, for example, often made the point that the unity of the family, which allowed it to act as an affectionate refuge from the harsh dog-eat-dog economic sphere, depended on there being one 'captain of the ship', and on the family having priority over the individuals within it (especially if that individual happened to be the wife). This was reflected in a married woman's lack of property rights and in her inability to hold jobs outside the home. So Mill needed to show, using sociological investigation, why families in which the partners were equal might nevertheless be stable.

Arguments against change in the role of women in the family did not only rely on claims about the conditions of social stability. They also grew out of theological or scientific arguments about the natural aptitudes, capacities and limitations of women. Answering the second objection against equality between the sexes, that women are not capable of being fundamentally different from how they already are, requires ethology, or the science of the effects of circumstances on character. Mill continually tries to undermine the very popular claim that a 'natural hierarchy' exists between men and women, rich and poor, by arguing that, given different circumstances, the weight of evidence suggests that the character of people in the 'subject group' could be very different – that it could include, for example, genuine moral agency. This serves to attack the foundations of paternalism (and should be seen, therefore, as a basic condition for the success of the project delineated in *On Liberty*).[19]

Mill starts by trying to debunk an opposing view that married life, rather than acting primarily to shape character, responds to the nature of men and women as it finds them. That is, he wants to attack the idea that institutions (and history more broadly) are merely containers for individuals determined by an invariant human nature. 'Standing on the ground of common sense and the constitution of the human mind, I deny that any one knows, or can know, the nature of the two sexes, as long as they have only been seen in their present relation to one another.'[20] The only way one could claim positive knowledge concerning the true nature of women would be if there had been societies of women without men or societies in which the women were not under the control of men. Then, by comparison, one might be able to make tentative determinations of the nature of women.

But Mill thinks it far more likely that '(w)hat is now called the nature of women is an eminently artificial thing – the result of forced repression in some directions, unnatural stimulation in others'.[21] This leads him to lament that '(o)f all difficulties which impede the progress of thought, and the formation of well-grounded opinions on life and social arrange-ments, the greatest is now the unspeakable ignorance and inattention of mankind in respect to the influences which form human character'.[22] That is, a gaping hole in human knowledge, one that allows for claims of the 'naturalness' of women's subordinate role, would only be addressed by an ethology: 'Whoever is in the least capable of estimating the influence on the mind of the entire domestic and social position and the whole habit of a life, must easily recognize in that influence a complete explanation of nearly all the apparent differences between women and men, including the whole of those which imply any inferiority.'[23]

No comprehensive ethology is forthcoming. But a central goal of *The Subjection of Women* (as well as of the *Principles of Political Economy*) involves defending various ethological claims. Mill wants to lay bare the impact of the family as presently constituted on the husbands, wives and bystanders (children), and imagines what the family and its members might be like if equality were its ruling principle.

Impact of Marriage on Women

The text pays special attention to the effects of marriage on women. Shocking his Victorian contemporaries, Mill consistently compares the subordination of women to the status held by slaves. But, given the legal status of wives mentioned earlier, this contention is not so far off. Women can own no property of their own. They must submit to the judgement of their husband, and to his sexual advances, whether desired or not. Any children are by law his rather than hers. And should a woman want to escape from an abusive marriage, she still finds the law on the side of the man, since, according to the Divorce Act of 1857, though the husband may divorce for adultery alone, the wife must prove incest, bigamy or extreme cruelty.[24]

Close attention to the impact of this legal and social subordination reveals a consistent pressure pushing the character of women towards selfishness and pettiness of vision on the one hand and towards self-annihilation on the other. Mill ends up trying to show how the current shape of the family generates gossip and causes the woman to be martyred to banality.

The figure of the martyr shines a revealing light on the relation of Mill's conception of character to his utilitarian commitments. Mill addresses the contemporary view that women are more 'susceptible of good feeling, and consideration for those with whom they are united by the strongest ties, than men are' by claiming that 'we are perpetually told that women are better than men, by those who are totally opposed to treating them as if they were as good; so that the saying has passed into a piece of tiresome cant, intended to put a complimentary face upon an injury'.[25] He goes on to suggest a less attractive candidate for female superiority: 'If women are better than men in anything, it surely is in individual self-sacrifice for those of their own family. But I lay little stress on this, so long as they are universally taught that they are born and created for self-sacrifice.'[26]

Sacrifice for the good of others still depends for its desirability on the manner in which the person undertakes the sacrifice. In the case of women, Mill thinks that the sacrifice comes from an 'exaggerated self-abnegation which is the present artificial ideal of feminine character',[27] a self-abnegation made possible by the belief, affirmed in small and big ways throughout daily life, that women's concerns come a distant second to men's.

The artificiality of the ideal can be contrasted with the ideals of the Religion of Humanity. In the latter case, one might engage in sacrifice for the sake of serving not only the individuals involved, but also one's conception of oneself as part of something great. A significant portion of the satisfaction that results derives from an ennobled sense of self, as, for example, helping the victory of good over evil in the Manichean struggle envisioned by Mill in his writings on religion. The self-sacrificing woman, however, lacks the moral glow of the religious martyr. She gives of herself automatically, because she has always done so. Her needs have become so intimately tied to and subordinated to the needs of those around her that she fails to have genuine desires of her own. She cannot affirm her choices because the possibility of doing otherwise never fully arises. In some sense, then, she makes no choice, and the act becomes something to pity rather than something to admire.

Mill also complains that the limitations of personal feeling and sympathy qualify the sacrifice of women. Rather than acting for the sake of a moral principle, which respects the value of all equally, women follow their inclinations to help only those they know. Mill contends that 'all the education which women receive from society inculcates on them the feeling that the individuals connected with them are the only ones to whom they owe any duty—the only ones whose interests they are called on to care for'.[28] Women 'are left strangers even to the elementary ideas which are presupposed in any intelligent regard for larger interests or higher moral objects'.[29]

We might connect this to our earlier discussions of the nature of the imagination. Whereas a lack of positive associations created through the absence of exposure to great art, history, poetry and philosophy can severely hinder the development of our moral imagination, the incessant limitation of the scope of a woman's legitimate interest – the restriction to marriage and keeping a home – cripples it. There can be little thought of the self-as-art, the self-as-something-to-be-perfected, when one's conceptions of the possibilities available remain so limited. A woman rarely sheds her identity as a woman, and that identity, as understood in the Victorian period, constricts her far more than any corset. Loosening this existential restriction for Mill involves both limiting the reach of 'woman' as an identifying category, i.e. making that category less determinative of action and interpretation (at least as long as the category retains negative implications), and providing an alternative, namely an expanded and ennobled category of 'human being' through which one's life may be understood.[30]

If self-abnegation does not consume a woman, her self-interested impulses frequently lead in harmful directions, because her conception of her own interest remains limited by her conception of reward and satisfaction. 'Society makes the whole life of a woman, in the easy classes, a continued self-sacrifice; it exacts from her an unremitting restraint of the whole of her natural inclinations, and the sole return it makes to her for what often deserves the name of a martyrdom, is consideration.'[31] Striving for consideration turns her constantly outward (like the lover of stories rather than the lover of poetry), and makes her much more prone to search for praise rather than praiseworthiness, which means that she seeks the praise of those near her, not of posterity or of the idealized community of humanity. This explains for Mill why so many women have achieved proficiency but not true mastery in so many arts: 'Women seldom have an eagerness for fame; they desire to be liked, loved, or admired by those whom they see with their eyes.'[32] This bespeaks a severe limitation of imagination. The absent can never move the woman whose training demands a constant attention to the present. The needs and demands of those around her consume her time and energy. Constituted by the horizons of her imagination, the horizons of her world extend no further than she can directly engage. Naturally, the praise and blame of those close to her, their expectations for what she ought to do and be, become all important to her.

An additional impediment to the cultivation of women rests in how they achieve consideration. Any consideration she receives from society depends less on her own actions and more on those of her husband. This prompts a woman to put all her energy into getting the right mate: 'Social circumstance makes it such that women, if they are to gain anything that they might want in the world, must do it through a man, and therefore, being attractive to men becomes the polar star of feminine education and formation of character.'[33] Thus women become hostages to whatever men and society at large value most in women. If expectations stop at pleasant conversation and appearance, competent musicianship, ability to run a home and have children, so do women's aspirations.

Impact of Marriage on Good and Bad Men

This situation creates special problems for the husband who loves virtue and who would brave public censure to do the right thing: 'The wife is the auxiliary of the common public opinion. A man who is married to a woman his inferior in intelligence, finds her a perpetual dead weight, or, worse than a dead weight, a drag, upon every aspiration of his to be better than public opinion requires him to be.'[34] If he wishes to act out of a sense of ethical responsibility at the price of public censure he runs into the opposition of his wife: 'Her consideration is inseparably connected with that of her husband, and after paying the full price for it, she finds that she is to lose it, for no reason of which she can feel the cogency. She has sacrificed her whole life to it, and her husband will not sacrifice it to a whim, a freak, an eccentricity; something not recognized or allowed for by the world, and which the world will agree with her in thinking a folly, if it thinks no worse!'[35] This condemnation applies even to more minor projects of self-cultivation which appear to take away from socially recognized goals and activities. Again, the world of the ordinary wife and the world of the cultivated husband – the communities with which they imaginatively and physically interact – have very few shared members or values. Yet, sensitive to the happiness of his wife, the good husband shrinks from inflicting pain on her even though it comes unaccompanied with malice or intention. As this continues over the years, consideration and his wife's happiness blunt the desire for self-cultivation or bring him to poignant regret. Moreover, as Mill's remarks to Comte emphasize, the inequality between spouses leads to imperfect bonds of affection.

A wonderful, full-blooded example of this set in the same period as Mill's text can be found in Edith Wharton's *The Age of Innocence*. Newland Archer, on European honeymoon with his eminently socially acceptable wife May, wishes to invite to dinner a French tutor whom he considers 'an interesting fellow' and with whom he had 'some awfully good talk after dinner about books and things', but whom May considers 'dreadfully common'. With a few sidelong, dismissive comments by May, Newland abandons the idea of meeting again with the man, with some relief, since the tutor expressed an interest in coming to Archer's hometown of New York. Immediately, however, this abandonment disturbs him:

> He perceived with a flash of chilling insight that in future many problems would be thus negatively solved for him; but as he paid the hansom and followed his wife's long train into the house he took refuge in the comforting platitude that the first six months were always the most difficult in marriage. 'After that I suppose we shall have pretty nearly finished rubbing off each other's angles', he reflected; but the worst of it was that May's pressure was already bearing on the very angles whose sharpness he most wanted to keep.[36]

Mill worries that when a real difference of ability exists in a marriage – a difference most often created by the culture of legal and social inequality – the man's 'self-satisfaction is incessantly ministered to on the one hand, on the other he insensibly imbibes the modes of feeling, and of looking at things, which belong to a more vulgar or a more limited mind than his own'.[37] Though a good man may not engage in self-worship, he does put aside projects of self-improvement, because he learns to be more and more satisfied with who he is (as long as he receives appropriate consideration from society). The constant dripping of his wife's words and actions wears his spirit down, smoothing him to inoffensive mediocrity.

Though a minor tragedy, damage to the hopes of good men like Archer exercises Mill's concern less than the brutalizing effects of unequal marriages on average and bad men. His claims here border on hyperbole, but include real insight: 'All the selfish propensities, the self-worship, the unjust self-preference, which exist among mankind, have their source and root in, and derive their principal nourishment from, the present consti-tution of the relation between men and women.'[38] This training starts from a very early age in the home and grows from the inequality of the relations between the sexes: 'Think what it is to be a boy, to grow up to manhood in the belief that without any merit or any exertion of his own, though he may be the most frivolous and empty or the most ignorant and stolid of mankind, by the mere fact of being born a male he is by right the superior of all and every one of an entire half of the human race.'[39] Mill goes on to ask, 'What must be the effect on his character of this lesson? And men of the cultivated classes are often not aware how deeply it sinks into the immense majority of male minds.'[40]

Mill gives a reasonably detailed report of the lessons learned by men. The implication of superiority pervades social life and infects the self-conception of boys, and he poses a basic question about it: 'Is it imagined that all this does not pervert the whole manner of existence of the man, both as an individual and as a social being?'[41] This master/slave or lord/vassal relationship, while it clearly impacts the slave, also does significant damage to the master's character. Mill constantly points out the unhealthy self-worship that a relationship of unmerited command over another promotes. It distorts one's judgement about the worth of one's actions and character. 'Human beings do not grow up from childhood in the possession of unearned distinctions, without pluming themselves upon them.'[42] Pride uncoupled from merit and attached to 'accidental advantages' fosters a propensity for 'arrogance and overbearingness'. And though social life with other men moderates these vices, this often means that the vices simply 'revenge themselves upon the unfortunate wife for the involuntary restraint which they are obliged to submit to elsewhere'.[43]

The effects of social relations on the affections thus take centre stage in Mill's account. Whereas relations among equals have a moderating effect on our passions as Adam Smith and others note, Mill asks about the impact of unequal relationships on self-conception and on affections. He concludes that the kind of power which 'present social institutions' give to husbands over wives 'seeks out and evokes the latent germs of selfishness in the remotest corners of [the husband's] nature' and 'offers to him a license for the indulgence of those points of his original character which in all other relations he would have found it necessary to repress and conceal, and the repression of which would in time have become a second nature'.[44] Social mechanisms of feedback and of tempering selfishness fail to function when one has learned to have little respect for one's audience. In this case, the female spectator, rather than moderating the man, often serves to provoke him. Any sense of impotence in other realms of life finds immediate relief when the husband commands his wife. Marriage represents a haven in which his needs get the attention he has come to feel that they deserve. Such a marriage makes a man self-indulgent and makes his wife miserable.

Mill expects a retort from opponents emphasizing the great love that exists within many marriages. This love, he claims, does nothing to turn aside his attack. The most unjust forms of domestic slavery often generate the most intense affections: 'It is part of the irony of life, that the strongest feelings of devoted gratitude of which human nature seems to be susceptible, are called forth in human beings towards those who, having the power entirely to crush their earthly existence, voluntarily refrain from using that power.'[45] Though character education should foster feelings like gratitude or desire for self-sacrifice, whether they can be considered virtues depends on their social context. In this case, the gratitude rests on a foundation of inequality, serves to reinforce that foundation, and also paints the relations that cause it in more attractive colours and tones.

This kind of gratitude in the modern world implies that the move from the law of force to the law of justice which characterizes social progress remains far too incomplete. 'The moral education of mankind has hitherto emanated chiefly from the law of force, and is adapted almost solely to the relations which force creates.'[46] At one time in humanity's historical development, political, social and economic requirements necessitated social relations adapted to the use of force. Force could not, as yet, be replaced by the rule of law. Regulation of behaviour by dint of individual strength and charisma stood in for obedience to general principles and institutions of justice. In these circumstances, gratitude of subordinate to superior served to cement the bonds of protection. In modern industrial society, however, the presence of 'devoted gratitude' expresses servility – a servility which no longer possesses the benefits it once did. The dangers and possibilities of modern society demand new individuals and new relationships. Traditional forms of marriage remain stuck in vestigial status, like the appendix. Their structure once served a social function, but that function diminished over time, and the justification for the form taken by the institution diminished with it.

Though 'existing moralities ... are mainly fitted to a relation of command and obedience ... command and obedience are but unfortunate necessities of human life: society in equality is its normal state'.[47] The growth of equal association, as Mill takes from Tocqueville and others, characterizes modern life. The 'morality of justice' represents the final stage in a growth from a morality of submission and through a morality of chivalry and generosity. We 'are entering into an order of things in which justice will again be the primary virtue; grounded as before on equal, but now also on sympathetic association; having its root no longer in the instinct of equals for self-protection, but in a cultivated sympathy between them; and no one being now left out, but an equal measure extended to all'.[48]

Conclusion

As *The Subjection of Women* shows, the malformation of the affections by inequalities in family structure presents a major obstacle to serious aesthetic education and can be addressed solely through institutional reform. Only relations regulated by principles of justice can provide the kind of education of the affections needed for modern men and women. 'The equality of married persons before the law, is not only the sole mode in which that particular relation can be made consistent with justice to both sides, and conducive to the happiness of both, but it is the only means of rendering the daily life of mankind, in any high sense, a school of moral cultivation.'[49] Mill's analysis of the effects of equality on character occupies a central place in his conception of the conditions which make internal culture possible.

The switch to relations constituted by justice remains difficult. Equality demands a steep price. It requires a new conception of the meaning of the relationship of husband and wife. Most prominently, it undercuts claims that the interests of the wife can be understood through the interests of the husband. This leads to the dissolution of the simple unity of the marriage state, for as Mill conceives of it, equality cannot mean that institutions trump and destroy individual personhood. The status of wife and the institution of the family cannot subsume and be prior to the status of person; rather, the priority has to be reversed. Wife derives from personhood – it doesn't destroy it. Securing personhood entails, among other things, securing separate property rights for the wife, and Mill knows that some people 'are sentimentally shocked at the idea of a separate interest in money matters, as inconsistent with the ideal fusion of two lives into one'.[50] But to base a community of goods on the principle that 'what is mine is yours but what is yours is not mine' flies in the face of justice.

For all the difficulties of achieving equality, and there are many, it yields significant dividends for the development of our affections and daily habits. First of all, it promotes sympathy. Those we consider equals – equals in moral status, equals in social position – are those with whom our imagination places us in closest contact, as we saw in Mill's comments to Comte. Implied by the presence of the power and obedience which characterize traditional relations between husband and wife are recognized differences that interfere with emotional contact. One becomes so familiar with one's role in life, whether as superior or inferior, that it becomes harder to imagine what it must be like to be in the other position. Equality mitigates this problem.

Secondly, equality in the family helps create the virtues 'which each requires to fit them for all other association'.[51] That is, the family would contribute to human progress by practising and making natural 'the same moral rule which is adapted to the normal constitution of human society'.[52] Mill never specifies what these virtues might be. He calls them the 'virtues of freedom', which presumably means that they are the qualities of character that further social life among equals. Rather than implying a social life grounded merely in contract and in low expectations for the benevolence of others (English life), the virtues promoted by the just family would seem to include softening tendencies. Included among them might be propensities to expect better of others in civil society (adding French sensibility to the structure of justice). This topic will come up again when we turn to Mill's discussion of the workplace and of industrial society.

Equality also reduces selfishness. Without it, the family reinforces self-worship in the husband: 'Any sentiment of freedom which can exist in a man whose nearest and dearest intimacies are with those of whom he is absolute master, is not the genuine or Christian love of freedom, but, what the love of freedom generally was in the ancients and in the middle ages—an intense feeling of the dignity and importance of his own personality.'[53] While inequality promotes valuing the husband's own projects and desires above those of the people around him, it also promotes the wife's 'artificial ideal' of self-abnegation. Her projects matter little in comparison to those of the master of the home. The habits and daily activities making up and emanating from a relationship based on mutual respect involve embracing a freedom that is not a mere lack of restraint, but one that finds itself in supporting others. It would seem that this kind of freedom depends upon realizing one's possibilities or nature as a being with social virtues and interests.

Both directly and indirectly, justice in the family also promotes the experience of higher pleasures. The ideal of marriage, involving mutual admiration and going beyond simple equality, is itself the basis for higher pleasures, namely the pleasures of exalted friendship. Higher pleasures also get indirect support, because the partners in an ideal marriage encourage each other's development: intellectual, aesthetic and moral. Admiring one's partner carries with it a desire to be admired by him or her. This basic impulse drives the propensity to look at one's life as the artist looks at something she creates – finding ways in which it can be made more perfect.

Lastly, and bringing us through the whole spectrum of aesthetic education's desiderata, we have the just family's power to inculcate an improved capacity of both men and women to forge an imaginative bond with an idealized humanity. One of the important conditions for this is the ability of individuals to identify themselves consistently as human beings. For Mill, though the moral idea of human being has a long history beginning in Rome and in Christianity, it remains uncommon for the identity to be primary. Daily life, particularly life in the family but also including class and religious differences, militates against that. Social identities (e.g. woman, man, worker, Catholic, Irishman, etc.) take up too much of our imaginative energy. The grip of these social identities has to be loosened if enough space is to be created for the morally preferable solidarity with others based on a shared humanity. To accomplish this requires a reformation of social institutions, with the family front and centre, but accompanied by the institutions which organize economic life. It is to these latter institutions that we shall turn our attention in the following chapter.

Endnotes

1. Raymond Williams, *Culture and Society 1780–1950* (New York: Columbia University Press, 1983), 62.
2. Collini contends that character was a pervasive concern in Victorian political discourse and that the ideal of character 'enjoyed a prominence in the political thought of the Victorian period that it had certainly not known before and that it has, arguably, not experienced since' (31). See Stefan Collini, 'The Idea of "Character" in Victorian Political Thought', *Transactions of the Royal Historical Society*, 5th series, 35 (1985), 29–50.
3. John Stuart Mill, *The Collected Works of John Stuart Mill*, gen. ed. John

M. Robson, 33 vols (Toronto: University of Toronto Press, 1963–91), XVIII:168–9.

4. Mill, *Collected Works*, XXI:295. An earlier (1820s) tradition of emphasis on the importance of social rather than political institutions is that of the Owenites. As Joanna Innes puts it: 'Disciples of Robert Owen were still more inclined to downgrade politics as an arena of struggle: to them, the key to change lay in a programme of "social reform", in a radical reordering of social relationships, above all in family, workplace, and neighbourhood' (93). See Joanna Innes, '"Reform" in English public life: the fortunes of a word' in *Rethinking the Age of Reform*, Arthur Burns and Joanna Innes (eds) (Cambridge: Cambridge University Press, 2003).

5. Mill, 'Michelet's History of France' [1844] in *Collected Works*, XX:232.

6. Ibid. Note the continuing use of inner/outer metaphors as discussed in Chapter 2.

7. Olive Anderson, 'State, Civil Society and Separation in Victorian Marriage', *Past and Present*, No. 163 (May 1999), 161–201.

8. See Mary Lyndon Shanley, 'Suffrage, Protective Labor Legislation, and Married Women's Property Laws in England', *Signs*, Vol. 12, No. 1 (1986), 74; and Janet Thomas, 'Women and Capitalism: Oppression or Emancipation? A Review Article', *Comparative Studies in Society and History*, Vol. 30, No. 3 (July 1988), 543.

9. Quoted in Mary Lyndon Shanely, 'Marital Slavery and Friendship: John Stuart Mill's *The Subjection of Women*', *Political Theory*, Vol. 9, No. 2 (May 1981), 232.

10. Quoted in Flavia Alaya, 'Victorian Science and the "Genius" of Woman', *Journal of the History of Ideas*, Vol. 38, No. 2 (April–June 1977), 265.

11. For historians who question the realization of this ideal in Victorian life, see M. Jeanne Peterson, 'No angels in the house: the Victorian myth and the Paget women', *American Historical Review*, Vol. 89, No. 3 (1984), 677–708; and Amanda Vickery, 'Golden Age to Separate Spheres? A Review of the Categories and Chronology of English Women's History', *The Historical Journal*, Vol. 36, No. 2 (June 1993), 383–414.

12. Shanley in 'Marital Slavery and Friendship' notes that Mill's position represents a significant break with the past. Many famous discussions of friendship (e.g. Montaigne, Aristotle, Hegel) and not so famous ones (e.g. Comte's letters to Mill) deny that women and men can be friends in the highest sense because there is a lack of equality between them.

13. Letter from John Stuart Mill to Auguste Comte, 13 July 1843, in *The Correspondence of John Stuart Mill and Auguste Comte*, translated from the French by Oscar A. Haac (New Brunswick, NJ: Transaction Publishers, 1995), 174. Comte's reply to this is fascinating and revealing: 'As to the

necessary imperfection of affections founded on inequality, I agree with you, and here I believe that the fullness of human sympathies could exist only between two eminent men whose moral stature is sufficient to restrain any serious impulse of rivalry. This kind of accord seems to me far superior to any that might ever exist between one sex and the other. However, this could obviously not be the normal type of the most basic and common relationships, where first the natural hierarchy of the sexes, then that of ages [i.e. generations], form the most powerful bond' (180).

14. Mill, *Collected Works*, XXVII:664.

15. Mill, *Collected Works*, XXI:261.

16. Mill and Comte, *Correspondence*, 174.

17. Mill, *Collected Works*, VIII:918.

18. Mill, *Collected Works*, VIII:919.

19. 'For there is, in the state of continuous, ever-present dependency, something that debilitates the soul and arrests any progress towards independence from the very start.' Mill and Comte, *Correspondence*, 202.

20. Mill, *Collected Works*, XXI:276.

21. Ibid.

22. Mill, *Collected Works*, XXI:277.

23. Mill, *Collected Works*, XXI:320.

24. See John Stuart Mill, *The Subjection of Women*, ed. Susan Okin (Indianapolis, IN: Hackett Publishing Company, 1988), 35 (note).

25. Mill, *Collected Works*, XXI:292–3.

26. Mill, *Collected Works*, XXI:293.

27. Ibid.

28. Mill, *Collected Works*, XXI:321.

29. Ibid.

30. In this, English women seem to have an advantage over those on the Continent: 'They [women] look upon themselves in our country, and men look at them, less as women and far more as human beings in general. True, their education imposes a number of special rules on their proper behaviour as women, but in the form of general principles, without any bearing on their position toward men, or toward a particular man. Social dependency hinders their development considerably, but does not affect it as much as in France.' Letter to Comte of 30 October 1843; in *Correspondence*, 200.

31. Mill, *Collected Works*, XXI:332. A close, historically sensitive class analysis of *The Subjection of Women* would go a long way to aiding an interpretation of the text. Much of the discussion implies women of the middle or upper classes, except where it turns to male violence and brutishness. How this shapes what Mill says is sometimes unclear.

32. Mill, *Collected Works*, XXI:320.

33. Mill, *Collected Works*, XXI:272.
34. Mill, *Collected Works*, XXI:332.
35. Ibid.
36. Edith Wharton, *The Age of Innocence* (New York: Macmillan Publishing Company, 1986), 204.
37. Mill, *Collected Works*, XXI:335.
38. Mill, *Collected Works*, XXI:324. It should be noted that Mill does not think that the habits acquired in the home are limited in expression to the roles in the home. The dispositions I pick up in this way are therefore *character* dispositions, not merely dispositions I have in my role as husband or son. The reach of habits beyond the context in which they originate is also implicit in Mill's discussions concerning the workplace. It may be a contestable point – one would have to look in detail at the acquisition and expression of habits.
39. Ibid.
40. Ibid.
41. Mill, *Collected Works*, XXI:324–5.
42. Mill, *Collected Works*, XXI:325. The negative impact of 'unearned distinction' is also a preoccupation of Mill's analysis of economic life.
43. Ibid.
44. Mill, *Collected Works*, XXI:289.
45. Mill, *Collected Works*, XXI:286–7.
46. Mill, *Collected Works*, XXI:293–4.
47. Mill, *Collected Works*, XXI:294.
48. Ibid.
49. Mill, *Collected Works*, XXI:293.
50. Mill, *Collected Works*, XXI:297.
51. Mill, *Collected Works*, XXI:295.
52. Ibid.
53. Ibid.

5

Social and Political Dimensions of Aesthetic Education:
The Industrial Economy and the Workplace

In his essay on Michelet, Mill praises the monastic associations of Italy and France after the reforms of St. Benedict: 'Unlike the useless communities of contemplative ascetics in the East, they were diligent in tilling the earth and fabricating useful products; they knew and taught that temporal work may also be a spiritual exercise.'[1] The transformation of temporal work into spiritual exercise can fruitfully be seen as Mill's most basic goal for reform of the workplace.

Turning the modern workplace into a place with spiritual value was a daunting task, however, as Adam Smith and later economists and social critics revealed. The division of labour, the growing size of factories and businesses (with the related de-personalization of work), the increasing simplicity and repetitiveness of the work, in other words the cornerstones of much of the economic success of modern Britain, all contributed to spiritual deadening – a limitation of emotional and imaginative reach or scope.

Coleridge expressed this more broadly in his contrast of mere 'civilization' with 'cultivation'. In his *On the Constitution of the Church and State According to the Idea of Each*, Coleridge claims that:

> The permanency of the nation ... and its progressiveness and personal freedom ... depend on a continuing and progressive civilization. But civilization is itself but a mixed good, if not far more a corrupting influence, the hectic of disease, not the bloom of health, and a nation so distinguished more fitly to be called a varnished than a polished people, where this civilization is not grounded in cultivation, in the harmonious development of those qualities and faculties that characterize our humanity. We must be men in order to be citizens.[2]

Civilization embodies modernity. It includes industrialism, cosmopolitanism, efficient bureaucracy, greater transience in population, a more urban and less rural nation, and greater material wealth (though often unevenly distributed). But civilization does little to support, and much to oppose, our spiritual or mental development.

Mill felt that the only way to address this pressing problem effectively in the realm of industry was through a fundamental reorganization of work. This reorganization would have the benefits of sufficiently maintaining or improving upon the efficiencies introduced by modern manufacturing, while providing spiritual sustenance for the workers. At the heart of this reform is Mill's advocacy for new relations of work which attempt to replace opposition of interests (often fostered by inequalities between workers and capitalists) with cooperation.

In this chapter, I shall examine three prominent and competing presentations of industrialism, along with Mill's criticisms of them (which tend to focus on their ethological and social statical inadequacies), in order to give adequate context for Mill's positions. We shall see that among the conservative and socialist critics of industrialism, one of the most prominent themes was the moral impact of work as it was then constituted. In particular, one of industrialism's greatest crimes was that it robbed social life of affection, sympathy and interest in the common good, by turning everything into contract and competition. I shall follow this with an account of Mill's take on industrialism, the workplace and the working classes, including his advocacy for industrial partnerships (on which he places his hopes for workplace cultivation of feeling and imagination), and conclude with some remarks on how cooperative forms of work were meant to promote aesthetic education. In particular, I am interested in showing how, for Mill, the activities and relations of economic life (especially in the workplace) needed to be reformed to provide for the possibility of situating one's labour in a more inspiring narrative than is available in unreformed economic life, and to show how the affections – those binding people to each other and to a common good – stand to be improved by this reform.

Views on Industrialization

Pro-industrialists

The first view concerning industrial society was that of the pro-industrialists who generally wanted things to continue on as they were going. In the *Principles of Political Economy*, Mill attacks that disposition (still present in contemporary political debate) which attaches 'inordinate importance ... to the mere increase of production'.[3] Proponents of this view tend to overlook, or to have no interest in, the potential for temporal work as spiritual exercise. Nor do they give enough weight to the possibility that the divisiveness and hostility of economic life as it exists could be otherwise.

Mill's goals for the organization of economic life are not exclusively material. If need be, he remains willing to trade material increase for forms of work that bring out and foster better character in the workers. A clear example of this can be found in his discussion of the stationary state (i.e. a state in which overall wealth is neither growing nor shrinking). Mill argues that the stationary state of capital and wealth should not garner the fear and aversion it does from 'political economists of the old school', and that, in fact, it should be something that reasonable people could welcome (as long as it accompanies a just distribution of wealth and static population growth). He confesses that he is not 'charmed with the ideal of life held out by those who think that the normal state of human beings is that of struggling to get on; that the trampling, crushing, elbowing, and treading on each other's heels, which form the existing type of social life, are the most desirable lot of human kind, or anything but the disagreeable symptoms of one of the phases of industrial progress'.[4] The conduct of industrial man is just that: the conduct of *industrial* man. This must be seen as a phase to be passed through, and humanity's shape in this phase should not be taken as expressing human nature in some full, ahistorical sense. Implicit in this criticism is Mill's confidence that the 'struggle for riches' need not predominate as a motive for action, that we can hope for a fundamental change in human motivations given a shift in social structure.[5]

This is not to say that the progressive state of industrial society that we must pass through to get to a stationary state does not serve a purpose. On the contrary, that 'the energies of mankind should be kept in employment by the struggle for riches, as they were formerly by the struggle of war, until the better minds succeed in educating the others into better things, is undoubtedly more desirable than that they should rust and stagnate. While minds are coarse they require coarse stimuli, and let them have them.'[6] This gives an interesting context to *On Liberty*'s emphasis on the need for energetic and active individuals. Free markets encourage certain kinds of activity, but not ones with which we should rest satisfied. Mill's emphasis on social institutions as fundamental in the development of character coupled with his different ideals of character yield a strong criticism of contemporary forms of capitalism.

Mill goes on to suggest that nineteenth-century advanced industrial societies are wealthy enough by far. 'It is only in the backward countries of the world that increased production is still an important object: in those most advanced, what is economically needed is a better distribution.'[7] Where wealth is properly distributed and stable, people will have turned their attention to other activities and goals than purely material ones. The best state for humanity is not one which encourages elbowing and trampling, but one in which 'while no one is poor, no one desires to be richer, nor has any reason to fear being thrust back, by the efforts of others to push themselves forward'.[8]

Conservatives

The second prominent position on the growth of industrialism and on the nature of industrial society was that of the conservative (as contrasted with the socialist) critics.[9] This strand of criticism is particularly important for our understanding of Mill's views on the workplace and its impact on aesthetic education because, though Mill agreed with conservatives concerning the need for a spiritual component to work (an 'anti-mechanism'), he takes them to task, as we shall see, for attempting to solve this problem through nostalgic appeal to hierarchy and paternalism.

Among the conservatives, one can identify three basic sets of criticisms. First, along with the socialists and others, they decried the dehumanizing nature of the work itself. It made people into little more than machines, severely limiting the development of their capacities.

Second, there was the problem of the anonymity of social life in modern industrial (especially urban) society. For example, I deal with the people in my local supermarket, not as a well-known individual with family, friends, a history, etc., but as a customer, as someone who has money and wants to exchange it for the pasta or apples on the shelves. Our relationship reduces to one dimension what had before been multidimensional. Public interaction of this sort increases my freedom because the participants limit their expectations for the interaction. It serves a very specific function: the exchange of goods for money. They don't know me and I don't know them. Unfortunately, increasing freedom in this way, by limiting what features of my personality and history are brought into an interaction, can liberate people to do questionable things. Deception becomes easier because we lack familiarity with each other – I may never see you again, and you have a much reduced capacity to hold me to account. Suspicion is engendered, and we retreat to the safety of contractual obligation in order to secure social stability. This anonymity, according to conservatives, exacerbates the growing lack of interest that people have in public life or in the well-being of others around them.

Third, these critics emphasize the hostility of worker/employer relations. The following passage from Carlyle's *Past and Present*, an excerpt of which was discussed in Chapter 3, is an outstanding and well-known representative of this complaint:

> True, it must be owned, we for the present, with our Mammon-Gospel, have come to strange conclusions. We call it a Society; and go about professing openly the totalest separation, isolation. Our life is not a mutual helpfulness; but rather, cloaked under due laws-of-war, named 'fair compensation' and so forth, it is a mutual hostility. We have profoundly forgotten everywhere that *Cash-payment* is not the sole relation of human beings; we think, nothing doubting, that it absolves and liquidates all engagements of man. 'My starving workers?' answers the rich mill-owner: 'Did not I hire them fairly in the market? Did I not pay them, to the last sixpence, the sum covenanted for? What have I to do with them more?' – Verily Mammon-worship is a melancholy creed. When Cain, for his own behoof had killed Abel, and was questioned, 'Where is thy brother?' he too made answer, 'Am I my brother's keeper?' Did I not pay my brother *his* wages, the thing he had merited from me?[10]

Isolation, contract, mutual hostility, the domination of social life by money – these became the standbys of critics. Carlyle helped to set the tone for discussions of the ethos of industrial society and for how to help the working classes who suffered most from that ethos.

How does one address these difficulties? Popular conservative answers tended to do two basic things. First, they called on the rich to go beyond contractual relations with the poor, to become their 'brother's keeper'.

In the best case scenario, this might mean turning capitalists into new incarnations of benevolent lords who took care of those for whom they were responsible.

Second, and related to the first point, there was a great interest in reducing anonymity through re-establishing more permanent, traditional relationships. An interesting and typical case is that of Francis William Newman, whose 1851 *Lectures on Political Economy* were reviewed that same year by Mill in the *Westminster Review*. Mill characterizes Newman's worries about the great evils of 'moral disorganization' as follows: 'His complaint is, virtually, that the old doctrines and old institutions do not continue. He complains that human beings are not bound together into fixed groups by an irrevocable bond; that hardly any of the relations of life are permanent; that people do not always hire the same labourers, buy and sell with the same persons, work for the same employers, and so forth.'[11]

One of the conservative recommendations here was to use legislation (e.g. Corn Laws) to preserve rural life while possibly encouraging a reverse migration from city to country. Agrarian life is a slower, less transient one, in which we know those with whom we deal. In addition, the virtues required of the farmer, though simple, are more admirable than those required of the merchant. Southey's discussion (treated in Chapter 3) of the difference between the quaint, tidy, well-apportioned rural home and the unhealthy, ugly, mass-produced dwellings of manufacturing society captures well this pro-rural, anti-urban outlook.[12]

Allied with the emphases on rural life, and part of the remedy for transient, anonymous relations, was the resurgence of medievalism in this period, since medieval life was taken as harking back to simpler times (times which were unmistakably rural). In the arts, for example, a gothic revival indicated the widespread interest in 'turning back the clock' to a better age.[13] The influence of medievalism on conservative reform is varied and not always direct, but it is certainly pervasive.

We can begin to understand Mill's criticisms of the conservatives and their efforts to assist the working classes by attending to the following: 'We yield to no one in our wish that "cash payment" should be no longer "the universal *nexus* between man and man;" that the employers and employed should have the feelings of friendly allies, not of hostile rivals whose gain is each other's loss. But while we agree, so far, with the new doctrines, it seems to us that some of those who preach them are looking in the wrong quarter for what they seek.'[14]

How exactly did these reformers look 'in the wrong quarter'? First of all, Mill thought that the paltry knowledge of political economy, so readily on display among critics like Southey, Coleridge and Carlyle, undercut the usefulness of their suggestions for reform. Very few of them had read any serious economists (with the partial exception of Malthus);[15] political economy for them was not important for what it taught, but for what it represented about the state of society. It rested on the assumption of self-interest, and disturbed the critics for the reflection it gave back to humanity. Our visage seems warped and ugly; it is without the features that inspire affection. Mill obviously dismisses this as superficial and dangerous avoidance of uncomfortable truth.

Second, and most importantly, Mill caught the stench of nostalgia. It was not that people were simply hoping to relieve distress. He interprets the interest of many of industrialism's critics to be much more far-reaching than that. New 'schemes of benevolence' are being 'propounded as instalments of a great social reform':

> They are celebrated as the beginning of a new moral order, or an old order revived, in which the possessors of property are to resume their place as the paternal guardians of those less fortunate; and which, when established, is to cause peace and union throughout society, and to extinguish, not indeed poverty – that hardly seems to be thought desirable – but the more abject forms of vice, destitution, and physical wretchedness.[16]

Attempting to ensure personal connection within economic life through 'an old order revived' ignores the ways in which relations must change to meet the new demands of history. It ignores, in other words, the truths of social statics and social dynamics. The railroad, for example, won't encourage permanence of social interaction, yet it cannot simply be thrown aside. The problems of the depersonalization of economic and social life cannot be addressed merely by attempting to freeze things as they were in an earlier century, particularly since this will rarely work to the advantage of the poor. Instead, we need to find new institutional forms – forms that reflect the realities of change.

As to those reformers, among whom Mill includes Carlyle, who focused on ensuring the well-being of the poor by calling upon the upper classes, he wonders if the reformers have seen the full implications of their paternalism:

It is quite possible to impose, as a moral or a legal obligation, upon the higher classes, that they shall be answerable for the well-doing and well-being of the lower. There have been times and places in which this has in some measure been done. States of society exist, in which it is the recognised duty of every owner of land, not only to see that all who dwell and work thereon are fed, clothed, and housed, in a sufficient manner; but to be, in so full a sense, responsible for their good conduct, as to indemnify all other persons for any damage they do, or offence they may commit. This must surely be the ideal state of society which the new philanthropists are contending for. Who are the happy labouring classes who enjoy the blessings of these wise ordinances? The Russian boors.[17]

With paternal care comes paternal authority. With paternal authority, we find the degradation of those cared for – they quickly lose their vigour and energy (a point established for Mill by ethological analysis and made famous in *On Liberty*). Mill puts a rather stark and questionable choice before us: 'There are but two modes of social existence for human beings: they must be left to the natural consequences of their mistakes in life; or society must guard against the mistakes by prevention or punishment.'[18] This applies to workers and women both.

Feudal society is gone, not to be recaptured. Re-emphasizing relations of protection and obedience will no longer produce affection and gratitude. There exist too many areas of life in which people have begun to demand equality of relations with others. They have become used to it, as Tocqueville's work brought home to Mill. Subordination now provokes resentment far more often than gratitude. Besides, 'Obedience in return for protection, is a bargain only made when protection can be had on no other terms. Men now make that bargain with society, not with an individual.'[19]

Though Mill recognizes the problem of social relations in industrialism, he does not believe that the anonymity of modern society can be addressed directly by forcing society back to an older, and by now outmoded, way of life. This is why the critics are looking in 'the wrong quarter'. Most efforts to make public life less impersonal invoke nostalgic images and are associated with medievalism and the continuing institutionalization of inequality. There is no way to rid ourselves of the hostility and anonymity of modernity from the top down. Our only hope is to build a commitment to the general interest in smaller institutional settings, thereby creating sympathetic and other affectionate links. This helps to explain why Mill focuses so much energy on how the workplace is structured.

Socialists

The third alternative for how society should be evaluated and changed came from the different brands of socialism. Since Mill considers himself a socialist, he is very concerned to differentiate himself from questionable socialist doctrines.[20] Mill summarizes his evaluation of socialism's main strength and weakness in an 1851 essay: 'Socialism, as long as it attacks the existing individualism, is easily triumphant; its weakness hitherto is in what it proposes to substitute.'[21] Mill's criticisms of socialism focused on two basic issues: 1) its attack on competition; and 2) a lack of gradualism in moral and social change.

While expressing agreement with many socialist critiques of industrial society and with some of their ideas for cooperative associations, Mill thinks they fail to appreciate the virtues of competition: '... I utterly dissent from the most conspicuous and vehement part of their teaching, their declamations against competition'.[22] The socialists mistake competition for the cause of the evils of the industrial system. 'They forget that wherever competition is not, monopoly is; and that monopoly, in all its forms, is the taxation of the industrious for the support of indolence, if not of plunder.'[23] Moreover, the only competition that can be said to hurt the workers, according to Mill, is that among labourers. All other competition benefits them by making the goods they need cheaper.

As for competition's moral impact, Mill admits that the socialists are not so far off when they argue that it promotes jealousy and hostility among those with the same occupation. But, 'if competition has its evils, it prevents greater evils'.[24] The common error of the socialists is 'to overlook the natural indolence of mankind; their tendency to be passive, to be the slaves of habit, to persist indefinitely in a course once chosen. Let them once attain any state of existence which they consider tolerable, and the danger to be apprehended is that they will thenceforth stagnate; will not exert themselves to improve, and by letting their faculties rust, will lose even the energy required to preserve them from deterioration.'[25] Competition is still a necessary stimulus for progress, and will remain so until someone can devise a better one.

It is telling how much emphasis Mill places on the importance of competition for human progress. Unlike many traditional accounts, which focus on the material benefits of competition, Mill's account concerns itself less with the purely economic advantages and more with moral ones. The concern for the conditions which shape our affections, desires and imaginations never wavers, and its horizon extends itself through civil society. As he puts it: 'To be protected against competition is to be protected in idleness, in mental dullness; to be saved the necessity of being as active and as intelligent as other people.'[26] This sheds an interesting new light on Mill's invocations in *On Liberty* of the need for energy and activity. To allow oneself to be blunted, to lose one's edge, is to forfeit one's individuality. The human propensity to wallow in comfort needs to be combated, and though the argument of *On Liberty* might suggest the spontaneous growth of individuality when certain social sanctions are lifted, Mill's criticisms of the socialists remind us that there are a number of positive requirements for the desirable forms of individuality as well. We cannot simply remove constraints on individuals and expect the best. People need to be pushed to improve.

The other basic mistake of many socialists is that they fail to appreciate how difficult fundamental change in human psychology can be. Socialism demands a great deal from members of the community, both in their moral development, broadly construed (i.e. their capacities to be motivated to labour for the community by the general interest and through feelings of duty and sympathy) and in their intellectual development (i.e. their abilities to estimate distant interests and discriminate good counsel from bad).[27] Mill declares that this 'entire renovation of the social fabric ... however valuable as an ideal, and even as a prophecy of ultimate possibilities, is not available as a present resource, since it requires from those who are to carry on the new order of things qualities both moral and intellectual, which require to be tested in all, and to be created in most; and this cannot be done by an Act of Parliament, but must be, on the most favourable supposition, a work of considerable time'.[28]

There exists a dialectical relationship between institutions and psychology, and each can advance only as far as the other will let it. The laws of social statics and social dynamics cannot be overstepped, and the particular history of a community involves commitments to various institutions and ways of life that will not stand for erasure. Mill suggests, instead, constant small-scale experimentation with socialist communities among society's intellectual and moral elite, with the dual goal of seeing whether socialism might work and, if it proves feasible, of training the next generation to be better suited for its rigours. This is especially important given the 'extreme moral unfitness' of the labouring classes 'for the rights which Socialism would confer & the duties it would impose'.[29]

Mill's vision of the workplace

Mill's account of the workplace as presently constituted

Mill's different critiques of industrialism recapitulate many of the points made by the conservatives and socialists while giving them a particular spin. He marks two problems for special consideration: 1) the lack of an apparent link between merit and success; and 2) an almost total absence of shared interests among workers themselves, and between workers and capitalists.

The tenuous connection of merit and success results from (and encourages) arbitrary inequalities of social status. Material reward 'instead of being proportioned to the labour and abstinence of the individual, is almost in an inverse ratio to it: those who receive the least, labour and abstain the most'.[30] Mill goes on to claim that the 'very idea of distributive justice, or of any proportionality between success and merit, or between success and exertion, is in the present state of society so manifestly chimerical as to be relegated to the regions of romance'.[31] This creates a situation in which vices like avarice and selfishness are often encouraged because virtues like honesty are reduced to being their own reward. As he warns elsewhere, 'Society educates the poor, for good or for ill, by its conduct to them, even more than by direct teaching.'[32]

The absence of a general or shared interest has negative effects on both economic and moral development. With economic development, since workers see their work as simply a means to collect wages, they will welcome inefficiency if their wages are not threatened. Public opinion among workers often encourages indolence: 'the rules of some trade societies actually forbid their members to exceed a certain standard of efficiency, lest they should diminish the number of labourers required for the work; and for the same reason they often violently resist contrivances for economizing labour'.[33] Somewhat ominously, Mill continues by arguing that the 'change from this to a state in which every person would have an interest in rendering every other person as industrious, skilful, and careful as possible ... would be a change very much for the better'.[34]

The moral impact of a workplace which does nothing to suggest common interest is profound. In his 'Chapters on Socialism', Mill suggests that the present-day, more 'far-sighted' socialists go beyond 'the mere levellers of former times' in their criticisms of society. In the eyes of the former, 'the very foundation of human life as at present constituted, the very principle on which the production and repartition of all material products is now carried on, is essentially vicious and anti-social. It is the principle of individualism, competition, each one for himself and against all the rest. It is grounded on opposition of interests, not harmony of interests, and under it every one is required to find his place by a struggle, by pushing others back or being pushed back by them.'[35] As we shall see, Mill is a bit more sanguine about the realities of industrial society. But though this is a starkly drawn picture, its basic outline is one he endorses. Indeed, it strongly resembles the account he gives of the deficiencies of English society in the *Autobiography* and in the 'Inaugural Address'.

If we are to overcome toxic forms of individualism, if 'public spirit, generous sentiments, or true justice and equality are desired', then 'associ-ation, not isolation, of interests, is the school in which these excellences are nurtured. The aim of improvement should be not solely to place human beings in a condition in which they will be able to do without one another, but to enable them to work with or for one another in relations not involving dependence.'[36] So the workplace, like the family, can act as a school for the affections and for different kinds of virtues, if power relations are configured to avoid overwhelming dependence. The principal way to make work into a school for the virtues rather than for the vices is through a reorganization of the workplace such that a common interest draws the attention and effort of the workers.

Industrial partnerships and aesthetic education

Like the conservatives and socialists, then, Mill wants to rid economic life of its hostility, making it more personal, affectionate and communal (and thereby making work much more amenable to becoming a form of 'spiritual activity'). He rejects many of their solutions, however, for a variety of ethological and social-statical reasons. The reformers often failed to see the implications of their plans for reform on character (including on habits of feeling and imagination) and/or they misunderstood what Mill takes to be basic truths (especially those of political economy) about social life.

Mill's solutions are attempts to mitigate the hostility of modern life and promote desirable dispositions of feeling and imagination by utilizing what he thinks are the best features of both capitalism and socialism. This finds expression in the following:

> Hitherto there has been no alternative for those who lived by their labour, but that of labouring either each for himself alone, or for a master. But the civilizing and improving influences of association, and the efficiency and economy of production on a large scale, may be obtained without dividing the producers into two parties with hostile interests and feelings, the many who do the work being mere servants under the command of the one who supplies the funds, and having no interest of their own in the enterprise except to earn their wages with as little labour as possible.[37]

The alternatives to dividing producers into hostile interests include two forms of partnership: 1) associations of labourers with capitalists; and 2) associations of labourers among themselves.

The first form of partnership, which, though it is less desirable, is more readily available, involves variations on the theme of profit-sharing. Mill often cites whaling ships and Cornish miners as examples. His favourite case study, however, is that of M. Leclaire, a Paris house-painter, who published an 1842 pamphlet detailing his method. Leclaire was dissatisfied with the conduct of his workforce and attempted to remedy the situation by simply raising wages. Though this served to minimize turnover, he found that unless he superintended every aspect of the work (which became impossible when his employees began to number in the hundreds) he could not depend on his employees to do a good job. His solution was to tie the workers' interests to the quality of the work by having them share in the profits. He made each worker a limited partner in the business.[38]

The second form of industrial partnership is one among the workers themselves. Ideally, such a combination would not just involve sharing profits (i.e. a form of limited partnership). Instead, it would entail the collective ownership of the capital (as articulated in the writings of Owen and Louis Blanc) and the guiding principle of these associations would be that they exist not for the 'mere private benefit of the individual members, but for the promotion of the cooperative cause'.[39] James Mill's friend, the Radical and tailor Francis Place, had organized some worker cooperatives, so perhaps Mill had been inspired by his example.[40]

Mill takes this to be potentially the best of all possible forms of economic organization yet devised. It combines economic advantages with moral ones. The economic advantages come in the form of increased productivity. Shared ownership of an enterprise gives 'vast stimulus ... to productive energies, by placing the labourers, as a mass, in a relation to their work which would make it their principle and their interest—at present it is neither—to do the utmost, instead of the least possible, in exchange for their remuneration'.[41] And though it is 'scarcely possible to rate too highly this material benefit' it is yet

as nothing compared with the moral revolution in society that would accompany it: the healing of the standing feud between capital and labour; the transformation of human life, from a conflict of classes struggling for opposite interests, to a friendly rivalry in the pursuit of a good common to all; the elevation of the dignity of labour; a new sense of security and independence in the labouring class; and the conversion of each human being's daily occupation into a school of the social sympathies and the practical intelligence.[42]

Mill imagines a new world, in which competition turns from clawing for material advantage to 'friendly rivalry' in pursuit of common goods. This may be too rosy a picture of human motivation to paint. Whether we can move from the 'coarse stimuli' of struggle for riches to a more noble state is something that Mill will admit is difficult to know. Possibilities for human motivation must be held in constant dialectical relation to empirical fact. Do we have the potential for 'friendly rivalry'? The pro-industrialists say no. The socialists say yes. It is something Mill asks that we remain open to.

We can now extrapolate to reach some conclusions about how Mill takes the reorganized workplace to promote the goals of aesthetic education – how, in other words, this work environment generates or fosters the dispositions that I have discussed in the previous chapters and that a traditional workplace fails to advance. First of all, we see that the notion of a 'school of the social sympathies' pops up yet again, as it did with discussions of the family. In order to work in a cooperative, we need to recognize shared interests. This recognition becomes institutionalized in partnership agreements, in the way money is distributed, in the work rules for the organization, etc. Institutionalization of shared interests thereby exerts consistent pressure on the members of the cooperative to identify with the cooperative and with the others who take part in it. This acts to reduce propensities to selfishness. By structuring the workplace and remuneration in this way, one turns dispositions of indifference or outright hostility into bonds of affection and solidarity.

This kind of institutional pressure scarcely exists in a traditional work environment. In the absence of unions, sympathetic connections are built, if they are at all, on the basis of shared passivity and commiseration, e.g. 'Our boss always makes demands for unpaid overtime ... isn't he/she horrible?' Sympathy in the cooperative is sympathy between agents who share a common project, not sympathy between patients. It serves, therefore, not only to increase connections among people, but also to constantly reinforce active, energetic self-understandings of the kind advocated in *On Liberty*. I come to see myself through the eyes of the institution and of the other members of the cooperative as someone who acts, not someone who is acted upon.[43]

Second, industrial cooperatives promote the 'dignity of labour' by connecting that labour to a common goal. This connection is made not only through institutional rules, but also through the imagination. Labour is transformed in a way similar to the transformation of history discussed in Chapter 3. History is no longer simply one thing after another; it represents a drama or epic to which each individual can contribute something, either good or bad. Just as the student of history is supposed to be brought into this way of viewing the past, the industrial cooperative moves the worker, through the mediation of the imagination, into seeing his or her work as part of something greater (thereby fostering the goals of the Religion of Humanity). It takes 'temporal work' and gives it the dignity of 'spiritual exercise'. I am not simply trading my time and labour for money. I am collecting money for doing something that I have additional, non-monetary motivations for doing. These non-monetary motivations (e.g. helping to achieve a common goal) are those which depend upon my imaginative identification with a collective.

These institutions also cultivate virtuous feelings like gratitude. As fewer work relationships depend upon the mastery and subordination which generates resentment and unhealthy feelings of attachment (e.g. of the slave for his master), and as fewer are merely affectively inert (e.g. the relations of independent wage-earners who happen to be in a shared physical space), there will be more opportunities for the natural development and exercise of virtues of affective response. If the cooperative functions well, there are more opportunities for the giving of favours among equals, thereby increasing the opportunities for evaluations of ingratitude and gratitude in comparison to an environment strictly dictated by 'cash payment'. We become more attuned, in other words, to how we give and receive favours than we would have been in other institutional settings. Other virtues get similar kinds of stimulus (e.g. loyalty).

Lastly, cooperative economic organization promotes various kinds of higher pleasures. There are the pleasures of friendship and of acting for a common good. There are pleasures associated with maintaining a sense of one's own dignity by emphasizing agency. And there are aesthetic pleasures, that is, imaginative associations with the ideal or infinite (e.g. the potential for idealization of work and of the workplace). The workplace becomes, in other words, imaginatively charged.

Conclusion

The analysis of the family and of economic organization has highlighted a number of things. First of all, we have seen the importance of, in Williams' words, the 'need for institutions which should confirm and constitute ... personal efforts'. Family and workplace contribute decisively, both positively and negatively, to the cultivation of character. The negative contributions find expression in many of Mill's criticisms against the Victorian family and workplace, in which ethological analyses reveal, for example, the shrivelling of sympathetic feelings due to inequality of power relations. These criticisms facilitate Mill's arguments for reform when coupled with the promises of the beneficial effects on character to be had from industrial partnerships and from marriage between admiring, equal friends. Central to the project of works like *The*

Subjection of Women and *Principles of Political Economy*, then, is painting as convincing and attractive an image as possible of the lives that we *could* lead under different, and reformed, institutional circumstances.

Second, we can see how the type of aesthetic education provided by the arts and poetic forms of philosophy, history, rhetoric, etc. is only part of the story of aesthetic education. Our habitual practices as constituted by institutional structure go a long way to giving form to our feelings and imaginings. Poetry does not and cannot do it alone. Individual moral development is intimately tied to communal development in the guise of social and political reform.

Next, we see in detail how Mill desires to support 'cultivation' without becoming an enemy of 'civilization'. We need not reject modernity and nostalgically celebrate medieval and rural life in order to guarantee character development. Institutions must be adapted to the demands of character development and draw on modernity's strengths, while recognizing on the basis of social-statical analysis that some features of modern society must be accepted. We cannot, for example, get rid of the growing anonymity of a number of formerly very personal relations (e.g. that between grocer and customer) without severely changing the course of economic development. We cannot slow down worker migration and expect to keep a nation of small towns. We cannot, without grave injustice, prevent women from becoming independent.

Lastly, and most importantly, Chapters 4 and 5 of this book advocate for a particular approach to understanding and evaluating Mill's ethical views – an approach which emphasizes the centrality of works like *The Subjection of Women* and *Principles of Political Economy* to Mill's ethical thought. For too long, commentators have thought that by focusing on the principle of utility or on the vague ideals for character discussed in *On Liberty* one could capture the essential elements of Mill's ethics. As I discussed in the Introduction, this is of little use if we want to know what it would be like to choose a Millian life and to live it. Mill's criticisms of these institutions and his recommendations for their reform go quite a long way, if we read them with the proper eye, in telling us what kind of day-to-day activity hinders or supports living a good life and having a good character by Mill's lights.

Endnotes

1. John Stuart Mill, 'Michelet's History of France' in *The Collected Works of John Stuart Mill*, gen. ed. John M. Robson, 33 vols (Toronto: University of Toronto Press, 1963–91), XX:240.

2. S. T. C. Coleridge, *On the Constitution of the Church and State According to the Idea of Each (3rd Edition), and Lay Sermons (2nd Edition)* (London: William Pickering, 1839), 46.

3. Mill, *Collected Works*, III:758.

4. Mill, *Collected Works*, III:754.

5. This indicates a basic division between Mill and the more 'realist', anti-perfectionist camp of Philosophic Radicalism represented by Bentham, which has little expectation that humans could be so different in their basic *motives* than they are now. Any differences could only be differences in *action* generated by a changing landscape of sanctions and by a more rational set of actors.

6. Mill, *Collected Works*, III:754.

7. Mill, *Collected Works*, III:755.

8. Ibid.

9. This was no organized 'school' of criticism as much as a very loose affiliation of like-minded thinkers.

10. Thomas Carlyle, *Past and Present* (London: Ward, Lock and Bowden, Ltd., 1897), 202–3.

11. Mill, 'Newman's Political Economy' in *Collected Works*, V:453.

12. Robert Southey, *Sir Thomas More: Or Colloquies on the Progress and Prospects of Society*, 2 vols (London: John Murray, 1829), I:173–4.

13. For an interesting account of the 'gothic spirit' in Victorian Britain and of its opposition to Hellenism, see Richard Jenkyns, *The Victorians and Ancient Greece* (Cambridge, MA: Harvard University Press, 1980).

14. Mill, 'The Claims of Labour' in *Collected Works*, IV:379.

15. Donald Winch, 'Introduction' in John Stuart Mill, *Principles of Political Economy: Books IV and V*, ed. Donald Winch (London: Penguin Classics, 1985), 18.

16. Mill, 'The Claims of Labour' in *Collected Works*, IV:373.

17. Ibid.

18. Mill, *Collected Works*, IV:374.

19. Mill, *Collected Works*, IV:380.

20. See, for example, his *Autobiography*.

21. Mill, 'Newman's Political Economy' in *Collected Works*, IV:444.

22. Mill, *Collected Works*, III:794.

23. Ibid.

24. Mill, *Collected Works*, III:795.
25. Ibid.
26. Ibid.
27. Mill, 'Chapters on Socialism' in *Collected Works*, V:746.
28. Mill, *Collected Works*, V:749–50.
29. Mill, *Collected Works*, XIV:84.
30. Mill, *Collected Works*, V:714.
31. Ibid. Mill continually brings to the reader's attention the moral problems associated with unearned distinctions. We saw its dangers with men, and he also finds it in the 'leisure classes'.
32. Mill, 'The Claims of Labour' in *Collected Works*, IV:379.
33. Mill, *Collected Works*, V:742.
34. Ibid.
35. Mill, *Collected Works*, V:715.
36. Mill, *Collected Works*, III:768.
37. Mill, *Collected Works*, III:768–9.
38. Mill, *Collected Works*, III:772–3. It should be noted that such arrangements were actually made impossible by English law until the middle of the nineteenth century, because any sharing of profits or investing of capital meant a sharing of liability up to all of one's assets. Mill's strong advocacy for industrial partnerships brought him to lobby for the passage of a number of pro-partnership laws. This lobbying included offering expert testimony to parliament on a number of occasions (the most relevant occasion is from 1850; see *Collected Works*, V:407–29).
39. Mill, *Collected Works*, III:783.
40. See Nicholas Capaldi, *John Stuart Mill: A Biography* (Cambridge: Cambridge University Press, 2004), 20.
41. Mill, *Collected Works*, III:792.
42. Ibid.
43. This self-understanding is not, primarily, an act of intellect. That is, it does not depend primarily on my perceiving new cause–effect relationships, though certainly I am aware of a factual difference between my new and old work environments and my new and old opportunities for agency. In thinking about how to describe the character of my life as a whole, there is no definitive fact to which I can refer. I am not making a cause–effect claim, I am trying to capture what distinguishes me. This largely depends, as far as I can see, on the quality of our imagination.

6

Conclusion

A P. B. S. series from the 1980s called *Ethics in America* opened every show with a graphic depicting four Greek pillars, each with a name at the top: 'Plato', 'Aristotle', 'Kant' and 'Mill'. This confirms in rather dramatic fashion Mill's place in the recent pantheon of ethicists – something further attested to by the high proportion of introductory ethics classes that include Mill's *Utilitarianism* along with Aristotle's *Nicomachean Ethics* and Kant's *Groundwork*. Mill's arguments concerning the principle of utility put him in that pantheon.[1]

It is interesting, therefore, to note that Mill did not attribute great practical importance to these arguments. In an early essay, after attacking the view that God's will grounds obligation, he says:

> But with regard to most of the other conflicting opinions respecting the primary grounds of moral obligation, it appears to us that a degree of importance is often attached to them, more than commensurate to the influence they really exercise for good or for evil. Doubtless they are important, as all questions in morals are important: a clear conception of the ultimate foundation of morality, is essential to a systematic and scientific treatment of the subject, and to the decision of some of its disputed practical problems. But the most momentous of the differences of opinion on the details of morality, have quite another origin. The real character of any man's ethical system depends not on his first and fundamental principle, which is of necessity so general as to be rarely susceptible of an immediate application to practice; but upon the nature of those secondary and intermediate maxims, *vera illa et media axiomata*, in which, as Bacon observes, real wisdom resides. The grand consideration is, not what any person regards as the ultimate end of human conduct, but through what intermediate ends he holds that his ultimate end is attainable, and should be pursued.[2]

Discovering the 'primary grounds of moral obligation' – the subject of so much debate between Kantians, utilitarians, and virtue ethicists

– ultimately satisfies intellectual rather than ethical needs. The meat of moral dispute is that of 'intermediate ends', including various ends for character (e.g. ideals, virtues, dispositions of imagination and feeling). Commitments to those ends, Mill suggests, do more to distinguish ethical views than allegiances to first principles. This implies that when people have differences of opinion in ethical matters, these differences do not depend principally on individuals' attachments to a particular ultimate ground for norms, but on their commitments to 'lower order' ends or principles (e.g. Bentham and Mill's shared commitment to the principle of utility does not prevent them from having very different systems of practical ethics). By Mill's own reckoning, then, understanding the 'real character' of his ethical system requires going beyond his arguments for the principle of utility to his treatment of more concrete intermediate ends. This book thereby rethinks Mill's ethics by looking through the lens provided by the most important of these intermediate ends, i.e. the goals for character education, rather than through the more traditional lens of arguments for the principle of utility.

As we have seen, character education is essential to Mill's version of utilitarianism because fostering overall happiness depends on the cultivation of people who both care about others and are capable of greater happiness for themselves. This cultivation is covered in a particular branch of character education: aesthetic education. Studying aesthetic education shows the types of 'intermediate ends' Mill advocated, the kind of conditions that help foster aesthetic education, and the nineteenth-century social, political, economic and intellectual contexts which assist us in making sense of his advocacy for it.

Among the 'intermediate ends' emphasized in aesthetic education, two are most important and garnered the most attention throughout this book. First, we find the utilitarian interest in promoting pleasure, not by just providing the right external environment (e.g. institutional setting), but by enhancing through 'internal culture' our capacities for experiencing pleasure and for defending our individuality in the face of the solvent effects of mass society. In particular, internal culture fosters aesthetic and sympathetic feelings, both of which are under threat from forces, like self-regard, intensified by industrial modernity. This goal of promoting aesthetic and sympathetic pleasures contrasts Mill's hedonism with 1) other forms of hedonism, such as traditional Epicureanism, that emphasize the avoidance of pain over developing new capacities for pleasure; and 2) those many variants of Victorian religious and secular thought that looked upon pleasure with the suspicion of those who felt humanity needed discipline rather than expansion.

Second, a basic moral desideratum for Mill is that we increase our feelings of connection to and concern for others. As many eighteenth- and nineteenth-century critics of utilitarianism pointed out, Bentham's reliance on self-interested actors fails to recognize the complexity of human motivation and the desirability of feeling more for our fellows than self-interest allows. The moral development Mill emphasizes thereby includes promoting feelings of solidarity with others, through, for example, encouraging institutional reform in the family and the workplace and through inculcating the compelling narratives of the Religion of Humanity. In this, he consistently rejects both the more conservative alternatives offered by people like Carlyle and Southey, which he felt were incompatible with justice and moral progress, and forms of socialism that failed to appreciate the value of competition and that had superficial theories of psychology and of social statics.

This study has opened up these intermediate ends of aesthetic education to philosophical analysis by careful reading of Mill's often vague prescriptions within their broader intellectual and social background. Such a reading makes Mill's positions more determinate and reveals Mill's *motivations* as an ethicist more clearly than when his writings are abstracted from their milieu and inserted into a grand philosophical debate of 'eternal questions'. This, in turn, indicates new areas in Mill's ethics for possible study, while revealing fresh ways in which Mill might have philosophical relevance for us, as someone who thought deeply about the impact of modernity on our ethical lives and about possibilities for individual and communal improvement.

Endnotes

1. Another contributing factor may be that *Utilitarianism* is short, clearly written, and has historical importance, thereby making it a convenient text for ethics classes.

2. Mill, 'Blakey's History of Moral Science' [1833] in *The Collected Works of John Stuart Mill*, gen. ed. John M. Robson, 33 vols (Toronto: University of Toronto Press, 1963–91), X:29. It should be noted that this is not an uncommon

position. Two 'religious utilitarians' of the eighteenth century – John Gay and John Brown – make similar points about the practical import of arguments for first principles, as do many others.

Bibliography

Abrams, M. H. *The Mirror and the Lamp: Romantic Theory and the Critical Tradition.* Oxford: Oxford University Press, 1953.

Abrams, M. H. *Natural Supernaturalism: Tradition and Revolution in Romantic Literature.* New York: W. W. Norton and Company, 1971.

Alaya, Flavia. 'Victorian Science and the "Genius" of Woman', *Journal of the History of Ideas*, Vol. 38, No. 2 (April–June 1977).

Alpers, Svetlana. 'Describe or Narrate? A Problem in Realistic Representation', *New Literary History 8*, #1, (Autumn 1976), 15–41.

Anderson, Olive. 'State, Civil Society and Separation in Victorian Marriage', *Past and Present*, No. 163 (May 1999), 161–201.

Arnold, Matthew. *Culture and Anarchy and other writings.* Cambridge: Cambridge University Press, 1993.

Beiser, Frederick. *Enlightenment, Revolution, & Romanticism.* Cambridge, MA: Harvard University Press, 1992.

Bentham, Jeremy. *The Works of Jeremy Bentham.* Edited by John Bowring. 10 vols. New York: Russell and Russell, 1962.

Bentham, Jeremy. *Deontology together with A Table of the Springs of Action and The Article on Utilitarianism.* Edited by Amnon Goldworth. Oxford: Clarendon Press, 1983.

Bentham, Jeremy. *An Introduction to the Principles of Morals and Legislation.* Oxford: Clarendon Press, 1996.

Berlin, Isaiah. *Four Essays on Liberty.* London: Oxford University Press, 1969.

Britton, Karl. 'John Stuart Mill on Christianity', in *James and John Stuart Mill: Papers of the Centenary Conference*, John Robson and Michael Laine (eds). Toronto: University of Toronto Press, 1976.

Burke, Edmund. *Reflections on the Revolution in France.* Edited by J. G. A. Pocock. Indianapolis, IN: Hackett Publishing Company, 1987.

Capaldi, Nicholas. *John Stuart Mill: A Biography.* Cambridge: Cambridge University Press, 2004.

Carlisle, Janice. *John Stuart Mill and the Writing of Character.* Athens, GA: University of Georgia Press, 1991.

Carlson, Allen. 'Appreciating art and appreciating nature', in *Landscape, natural beauty and the arts*, edited by Salim Kemal and Ivan Gaskell, 199–227. Cambridge: Cambridge University Press, 1993.

Carlyle, Thomas. *Critical and Miscellaneous Essays.* Philadelphia, PA: Casey and Hart, 1845.

Carlyle, Thomas. *Past and Present*. London: Ward, Lock, and Bowden, Ltd., 1897.

Carlyle, Thomas. *A Carlyle Reader*. Edited by G. B. Tennyson. Cambridge: Cambridge University Press, 1984.

Coleridge, S. T. C. *On the Constitution of the Church and State According to the Idea of Each (3rd Edition), and Lay Sermons (2nd Edition)*. London: William Pickering, 1839.

Collini, Stefan. 'The Idea of "Character" in Victorian Political Thought', *Transactions of the Royal Historical Society*, 5th series, 35 (1985), 29–50.

Collini, Stefan. *Public Moralists, Political Thought and Intellectual Life in Great Britain 1850–1930*. Oxford: Clarendon Press, 1991.

Collini, Stefan, Donald Winch, and John Burrow. *That Noble Science of Politics: A Study in Nineteenth-century Intellectual History*. Cambridge: Cambridge University Press, 1983.

Comte, Auguste. *A General View of Positivism*. 1848. Reprint. Dubuque, IA: Brown Reprints, 1971.

Crafts, N. F. R. 'Some Dimensions of the "Quality of Life" during the British Industrial Revolution', *The Economic History Review*, Vol. 50, No. 4 (November 1997), 617–39.

Crafts, N. F. R. 'Forging Ahead and Falling Behind: The Rise and Relative Decline of the First Industrial Nation', *The Journal of Economic Perspectives*, Vol. 12, No. 2 (Spring 1998), 193–210.

Crimmins, James E. *Secular Utilitarianism: Social Science and the Critique of Religion in the Thought of Jeremy Bentham*. Oxford: Clarendon Press, 1990.

Curtin, Michael. 'A Question of Manners: Status and Gender in Etiquette and Courtesy', *Journal of Modern History* 57 (September 1985), 395–423.

Donner, Wendy. *The Liberal Self: John Stuart Mill's Moral and Political Philosophy*. Ithaca, NY: Cornell University Press, 1991.

Durkheim, Emile. *The Rules of Sociological Method*. New York: The Free Press, 1982.

Eagleton, Terry. *The Ideology of the Aesthetic*. Oxford: Blackwell Publishing, 1990.

Eagleton, Terry. 'Sweetness and Light for all', *Times Literary Supplement*, 21 January 2000, 14–15.

Elias, Norbert. *The Civilizing Process*. Oxford: Blackwell Publishing, 1994.

Epictetus. *The Encheiridion*. Translated by Nicholas P. White. Indianapolis, IN: Hackett Publishing, 1983.

Feagin, Susan. 'Mill and Edwards on the Higher Pleasures', *Philosophy* 58 (1983), 244–52.

Feinstein, Charles H. 'Pessimism Perpetuated: Real Wages and the Standard of Living in Britain during and after the Industrial Revolution', *The Journal of Economic History*, Vol. 58, No. 3 (September 1998), 625–58.

Fried, Michael. *Absorption and Theatricality: Painting and Beholder in the Age of Diderot.* Berkeley, CA: University of California Press, 1980.

Genette, Gerard. 'Boundaries of Narrative', *New Literary History 8*, #1 (Autumn 1976), 1–13.

Gombrich, E. H. *Art and Illusion.* Princeton, NJ: Princeton University Press, 1961.

Gray, John. *Hayek on Liberty*, 3rd edition. London: Routledge, 1998.

Haakonssen, Knud. *Natural Law and Moral Philosophy.* Cambridge: Cambridge University Press, 1996.

Halevy, Elie. *The Growth of Philosophical Radicalism.* Translated by Mary Morris. Boston, MA: Beacon Press, 1955.

Hamburger, Joseph. 'Religion and "On Liberty"', in *A Cultivated Mind: Essays on J. S. Mill Presented to John M. Robson*, edited by Michael Laine, 139–81. Toronto: University of Toronto Press, 1961.

Hamowy, Ronald. *The Scottish Enlightenment and the Theory of Spontaneous Order.* Carbondale, KS: Southern Illinois University Press, 1987.

Harris, Wendell. 'Ruskin's Theoretic Practicality and the Royal Academy's Aesthetic Idealism', *Nineteenth-Century Literature*, Vol. 52, No. 1 (June 1997), 80–102.

Harrison, Brian. 'State Intervention and Moral Reform in Nineteeth-century England', in *Pressure from Without in Early Victorian England*, edited by Patricia Hollis, 289–322. New York: St. Martin's Press, 1974.

Harrison, Ross. *Bentham.* London: Routledge and Kegan Paul, 1983.

Hedley, Douglas. *Coleridge, Philosophy and Religion: Aids to Reflection and the Mirror of the Spirit.* Cambridge: Cambridge University Press, 2000.

Helvetius, Claude-Adrien. *De L'Esprit.* Tours: Librairie Artheme Fayard, 1988.

Home, Henry (Lord Kames). *Essays on the Principles of Morality and Natural Religion.* Indianapolis, IN: Liberty Fund, 2005.

Hoock, Holger. 'Reforming culture: national art institutions in the age of reform', in *Rethinking the Age of Reform*, Burns and Innes (eds), 254–70. Cambridge: Cambridge University Press, 2003.

Humboldt, Wilhelm von. *The Limits of State Action.* Translated by John Burrow. Indianapolis, IN: Liberty Fund, 1993.

Innes, Joanna. '"Reform" in English public life: the fortunes of a word', in *Rethinking the Age of Reform*, Arthur Burns and Joanna Innes (eds). Cambridge: Cambridge University Press, 2003.

Jenkyns, Richard. *The Victorians and Ancient Greece.* Cambridge, MA: Harvard University Press, 1980.

Jones, H. S. 'John Stuart Mill as Moralist', *Journal of the History of Ideas*, 53 (1992), 287–308.

Kant, Immanuel. *Critique of Judgment*. Indianapolis: IN: Hackett Publishing Company, 1987.

Kant, Immanuel. *Critique of Practical Reason*. Cambridge: Cambridge University Press, 1997.

Kearney, Richard. *On Stories*. London: Routledge, 2002.

Kosman, L. A. 'On Being Properly Affected', in *Essays on Aristotle's Ethics*, edited by Amelie Rorty, 103–16. Berkeley, CA: University of California Press, 1980.

Lecky, William. *History of the Rise and Influence of the Spirit of Rationalism in Europe*. New York: D. Appleton and Company, 1888.

Louch, A. R. 'Criticism and Theory', *New Literary History 8*, #1 (Autumn 1976), 171–82.

Macaulay, Thomas. *Critical and Historical Essays*, 2 vols. London: Everyman's Library, 1937.

MacIntyre, Alasdair. *After Virtue*, 2nd edition. Notre Dame, IN: University of Notre Dame Press, 1984.

Mackintosh, James. *Dissertation Second; Exhibiting a General View of the Progress of Ethical Philosophy, Chiefly During the Seventeenth and Eighteenth Centuries*. Prefixed to the seventh edition of the Encyclopedia Britannica. 1830.

Mandelbaum, Maurice. *History, Man and Reason*. Baltimore, MD: Johns Hopkins University Press, 1971.

Mandelbaum, Maurice. *Phenomenology of Moral Experience*. Baltimore, MD: Johns Hopkins University Press, 1969.

Matz, Lou. 'The Utility of Religious Illusion: A Critique of J. S. Mill's Religion of Humanity', *Utilitas* 12 (2000), 137–54.

Mill, James. *An Analysis of the Phenomena of the Human Mind*. Edited and with notes by John Stuart Mill. London: Longmans, Green and Dyer, 1869.

Mill, John Stuart. *A System of Logic*. New York: Harper & Brothers, 1874.

Mill, John Stuart. *The Collected Works of John Stuart Mill*. Gen. ed. John M. Robson. 33 vols. Toronto: University of Toronto Press, 1963–91.

Mill, John Stuart. *The Subjection of Women*. Edited by Susan Okin. Indianapolis, IN: Hackett Publishing Company, 1988.

Mill, John Stuart and Auguste Comte. *The Correspondence of John Stuart Mill and Auguste Comte*. Translated from the French by Oscar A. Haac. New Brunswick, NJ: Transaction Publishers, 1995.

Mill, John Stuart and Jeremy Bentham. *Utilitarianism and Other Essays*. Edited by Alan Ryan. London: Penguin Books, 1987.

Millar, Alan. 'Mill on Religion', in *The Cambridge Companion to Mill*, John Skorupski (ed.). Cambridge: Cambridge University Press, 1998.

Norton, Robert E. *The Beautiful Soul: Aesthetic Morality in the Eighteenth Century.* Ithaca, NY: Cornell University Press, 1995.

Packe, Michael. *The Life of John Stuart Mill.* New York: Macmillan Company, 1954.

Passmore, John. *The Perfectibility of Man.* New York: Charles Scribner's Sons, 1970.

Peterson, M. Jeanne. 'No angels in the house: the Victorian myth and the Paget women', *American Historical Review*, Vol. 89, No. 3 (1984), 677–708.

Plotinus. *The Enneads.* Translated by Stephen MacKenna. New York: Penguin Books, 1991.

Raeder, Linda C. *John Stuart Mill and the Religion of Humanity.* Columbia, MO: University of Missouri Press, 2002.

Robson, John M. *The Improvement of Mankind: The Social and Political Thought of John Stuart Mill.* Toronto: Toronto University Press, 1968.

Robson, John. 'J. S. Mill's Theory of Poetry', in *Mill: A Collection of Critical Essays*, J. B. Schneewind (ed.). London: Macmillan, 1968.

Rorty, Richard. *Contingency, Irony, and Solidarity.* Cambridge: Cambridge University Press, 1989.

Ruskin, John. *Modern Painters.* Vol. 2. New York: D. D. Merrill Company, 1893.

Ryan, Alan. *The Philosophy of John Stuart Mill.* London: Macmillan, 1970.

Ryan, Alan. *J. S. Mill.* London: Routledge and Kegan Paul, 1974.

Schneewind, J. B. *Sidgwick's Ethics and Victorian Moral Philosophy.* Oxford: Clarendon Press, 1977.

Schopenhauer, Arthur. *On the Basis of Morality.* Indianapolis, IN: Hackett Publishing Company, 1995.

Sen, Amartya, and Bernard Williams (eds). *Utilitarianism and Beyond.* Cambridge: Cambridge University Press, 1982.

Seneca. *Moral and Political Essays.* Edited and translated by John M. Cooper and J. F. Procope. Cambridge: Cambridge University Press, 1995.

Shanely, Mary Lyndon. 'Marital Slavery and Friendship: John Stuart Mill's *The Subjection of Women*', *Political Theory*, Vol. 9, No. 2 (May 1981), 229–47.

Shanley, Mary Lyndon. 'Suffrage, Protective Labor Legislation, and Married Women's Property Laws in England', *Signs*, Vol. 12, No. 1 (1986).

Sharpless, F. Parvin. *The Literary Criticism of John Stuart Mill.* The Hague: Mouton & Co., 1967.

Shrimpton, Nicholas. 'Ruskin and the Aesthetes', in *Ruskin and the Dawn of the Modern*, ed. Dinah Birch, 134–5. Oxford: Oxford University Press, 1999.

Sidgwick, Henry. *Methods of Ethics.* Indianapolis, IN: Hackett Publishing Company, 1981.

Skorupski, John. *John Stuart Mill.* London: Routledge, 1989.

Skorupski, John. 'Introduction', in *The Cambridge Companion to Mill*. Edited by John Skorupski. Cambridge: Cambridge University Press, 1998.

Smart, J. J. C. 'Extreme and Restricted Utilitarianism', *The Philosophical Quarterly*, (October 1956), 344–54.

Smith, Adam. *An Inquiry into the Nature and Causes of the Wealth of Nations*. Gen. eds Cambell and Skinner, 2 vols. Indianapolis, IN: Liberty Press, 1981.

Smith, Adam. *The Theory of Moral Sentiments*. Indianapolis, IN: Liberty Classics, 1982.

Southey, Robert. *Sir Thomas More: Or Colloquies on the Progress and Prospects of Society*. Vol. 1. London: John Murray, 1829.

Stewart, Robert Scott. 'Mill's Theory of Imagination', *History of Philosophy Quarterly*, Vol. 10, No. 4 (1993), 369–88.

Sussman, Herbert. *Victorians and the Machine*. Cambridge, MA: Harvard University Press, 1968.

Thomas, Janet. 'Women and Capitalism: Oppression or Emancipation? A Review Article', *Comparative Studies in Society and History*, Vol. 30, No. 3 (July 1988).

Thomas, William. *The Philosophic Radicals: Nine Studies in Theory and Practice 1817–1841*. Oxford: Clarendon Press, 1979.

Urmson, J. O. 'The Interpretation of the Moral Philosophy of J. S. Mill', *The Philosophical Quarterly* (January 1953), 33–9.

Vickery, Amanda. 'Golden Age to Separate Spheres? A Review of the Categories and Chronology of English Women's History', *The Historical Journal*, Vol. 36, No. 2 (June 1993), 383–414.

Vogler, Candace. *John Stuart Mill's Deliberative Landscape*. New York: Garland Publishing, 2001.

Wernick, Andrew. *Auguste Comte and the Religion of Humanity*. Cambridge: Cambridge University Press, 2001.

Wharton, Edith. *The Age of Innocence*. New York: Macmillian Publishing Company, 1986.

Whewell, William. *Lectures on the History of Moral Philosophy in England*. London: Thoemmes Antiquarian Books Ltd., 1990.

Williams, Raymond. *Culture and Society 1780–1950*. New York: Columbia University Press, 1983.

Wilson, F. *Psychological Analysis and the Philosophy of John Stuart Mill*. Toronto: Toronto University Press, 1990.

Wright, T. R. *The Religion of Humanity: The Impact of Comtean Positivism on Victorian Britain*. Cambridge: Cambridge University Press, 1986.

Index